CONCILIUM

concilium 1996/4

PILGRIMAGE

Edited by

Virgil Elizondo and
Sean Freyne

SCM Press · London

Orbis Books · Maryknoll

Published by SCM Press Ltd, 9–17 St Albans Place, London N1
and by Orbis Books, Maryknoll, NY 10545

ISBN: 0 334 03039 0 (UK)
ISBN: 1 57075 073 4 (USA)

Typeset at The Spartan Press Ltd, Lymington, Hants
Printed by Mackays of Chatham, Kent

Concilium Published February, April, June, August, October, December.

Contents

Introduction

Pilgrimage: An Enduring Ritual of Humanity

On any average day of the year, while many of the churches of the Christian world remain quite empty, pilgrims from all walks of life flock to pilgrimage sites seeking something beyond what they are receiving in their home churches or university classrooms – 20,000 a day at Lourdes in Europe or at Tepeyac in the Americas, and similar numbers at other pilgrimage sites throughout the world. Around the Feast of Our Lady of Guadalupe on 12 December it is estimated that well over 2 million pilgrims visit her shrine at Tepeyac. In 1993, 70,000 'pilgrim's certificates' indicating that the person had walked at least 100 kilometres along the medieval pilgrim's path were issued at Compostela in Spain – up from only 2,000 in 1983. In a recent article in the *New York Times*, the Revd Michel de Roton, rector of the shrine at Lourdes, was quoted as saying: 'You'd think that in our time the pilgrimage would have faded away. But pilgrimages are definitely growing. They seem to fulfil a need of the soul . . . Perhaps people find religious life too monotonous and want something more intense, more festive, more emotional. Perhaps the form religion has taken today does not correspond to people's needs.'[1] This is happening not only within the Christian world, but within other religions as well.

In the midst of growing secularism and modernity, technology and electronics, mobility and rapid travel, space exploration and information super-highways, people are seeking the stable and unchanging rootedness of sacred earth. The faster humanity moves, the more it needs to be grounded. It seems that pilgrimage sites are responding to this deep anthropological need of the human soul to be connected to mother earth. Furthermore, the more knowledge, science and information we have, the greater the quest of the soul for ultimate meaning; the more psychological analysis and psychotherapy we undergo, the greater the quest of the soul for penance and purification; the more medical science accomplishes, the greater the search for miracles; and the more families break apart while churches become more rule-orientated, the greater the quest for an unconditional human community.

People go on pilgrimage seeking and hoping to find what their present world – modern or ancient – has not been able to offer them. The ritual and mystery of pilgrimage is so consistent throughout the history of humanity, regardless of the changes and advances civilizations make, that it almost appears to be grounded on the very biological genes which make us human!

Pilgrimage sites attract the tourist and the pilgrim, the young and the old, the healthy and the sickly, families and individuals, the devout and the curious, the alms-giver and the pick-pocket, the soul-searching and the vendor. The very nature of the pilgrimage allows ordinary social divisions to fade out as the great diversity of pilgrims experience a common bond based on the unifying experience of the pilgrimage. The pilgrimage itself mirrors not only the most basic reality of the church, the people of God on the pilgrimage of life, but even more so the reality of humanity itself, human beings together on the way to the mysterious beyond. Something of this mysterious beyond of humanity can be seen and experienced within the pilgrimage. The peaceful and harmonious mixture of peoples from all classes, ethnicities and races which gather together at the pilgrimage site can certainly be an image and foretaste of the ideal humanity of the future, one which is already beginning, but usually in much turmoil, conflict, resistance and even bloodshed: the multi-racial and multi-cultural reality of today's world. The church, like the world, is becoming a multi-racial and multi-cultural grouping of peoples within every parish or city: will we end up fighting each other for the same space, or create a new family inclusive of all of us within the same space?

Pilgrimage sites are privileged earth-places where one can recall and thus make present in one's own life the great interventions of God on earth and within human history. In these moments, one can come into a more personal knowledge of and communion with the great wonders of God in nature such as Sinai, Kailâsa and Mânasaras and/or in the very simple human beings through whom God has spoken and acted, such as the shepherds in Fatima or Juan Diego in Tepeyac, or more immediately, the testimonies of persons whom one meets on the way. Even in the Holy Land one comes into personal contact not with the divinity of Christ, but with elements of the earthly Jesus of Nazareth who was born of a woman in a rural area, lived among ordinary people, worked for a living, struggled with his calling and with the people around him, taught in the synagogues and open spaces, was crucified as a criminal and was buried in a borrowed plot.

Pilgrimage sites break away from the recognized centres of organized religion and from the control of their authorities. Maybe they can be attributed to God's sense of humour which keeps legitimate authority – whether ecclesial or academic – from taking itself so seriously that it confuses itself with God. Pilgrimages are not against official religion and its legitimate authority, and usually even bring new life into it; they are simply God's way of keeping authority humble by demonstrating through the mediation of the poor and the lowly that God's tenderness knows no bounds and that God continues to disregard all human criteria and evaluations in choosing God's special messengers to humanity.[2] Thus they witness to the limits of any official religion or theology which tries to corral and imprison the mysterious infinity of God's love as it continues to be made manifest amongst us through the poor, the needy, the lowly and the unauthorized of society.

Pilgrimages expand and enrich the limits of our ordinary world-vision. People come from a multiplicity of cultures, backgrounds, ages and personal situations. Yet they all come of their own accord, searching for something beyond the ordinary. There is no church mandate which prescribes pilgrimages, yet the number of people going on pilgrimages continues to increase, while attendance at church-mandated services continues to decline. The sense of pilgrimage seems to respond to a profound need of the human being to go beyond the limits of ordinary experience into the mysterious realm of the beyond, and pilgrimage sites seem to have the force of a geographical biological-spiritual magnet attracting the pilgrims into the realm of its life-giving mystery. Yet pilgrimage sites are not ends in themselves, but often serve as thresholds into new stages of life. One does not go as a pilgrim to stay, but to pass through a privileged experience that will change us in unsuspected and uncontrolled ways so that we return to ordinary life in a completely new way. One breaks through limitations to experience a bit more of the ultimate and unlimited existence.

The attractiveness of sacred sites makes them privileged places for religious commercialism, and in many ways the merchants respond to the needs and desires of the pilgrims for lodging, food, entertainment, mementos, candle-offerings and souvenirs. This cannot be avoided, and can actually be a service in the overall function of the pilgrimage site.

Unfortunately, often the commercial aspect seems to outdo (outshine) the religious and spiritual purpose of pilgrimages when more emphasis is given to monetary offering and the sale of religious objects than to the pastoral care of pilgrims. Yet the abuse does not destroy the potential for making pilgrimage sites privileged places of encounter with the ultimate: encounters with oneself, with life, with others, with history, with nature, with the cosmos and with God.

Pilgrimages are an increasing fact of life, not just for Christians but for humanity. Far from disappearing from our modern world, they are increasing – greater numbers are flocking to the traditional sites such as the Holy Land, Compostela (Spain) or Tepeyac (Mexico), and new ones such as Lourdes, Fatima, Taizé, and Medjugorge. The Protestant Reformation and the Enlightenment regarded them as useless and childish, while post-Vatican II cerebral Catholicism has tended to play down their importance, yet people of all walks of life and of all religions are going on pilgrimage in ever-increasing numbers. This number of *Concilium* will seek to study this universal phenomenon which links ancient traditions with modern and post-modern ones.

Virgil Elizondo

Notes

1. Marlise Simons, 'Pilgrims Crowding Europe's Catholic Shrines', *The New York Times*, 12 October 1993.

2. Virgil Elizondo, *La Morenita, Evangelizer of the Americas*, Mexican American Cultural Center, San Antonio, Texas 1980 and subsequent articles in *Concilium* 122 and 128.

The Modern Pilgrim: A Christian Ritual Between Tradition and Post-Modernity

Paul Post

I. The paradox of the crisis in Christian ritual

Various liturgists and experts on ritual have pointed to what is termed the so-called 'paradox of the crisis in ritual' in Europe and the United States. On the one hand, questions are being asked with increasing urgency about the inculturation of rituals. But at the same time, unexpectedly and often outside the sphere of the organized church, on the other hand there is an enormous interest in rituals and symbols. Here, at numerous points, the 'traditional' Christian liturgical repertoire seems to be playing a part. In many places there is a flowering of rituals, public and private, which also – according to research – includes rituals from popular religious culture. In this context, which is of the utmost importance for liturgical studies, it is fitting to pay some attention to the often forgotten themes of pilgrimages and devotions.

For some years now pilgrimage has figured in the research agenda of liturgical studies in The Netherlands, and questions relating to it have been raised within the broader framework of an interest in innovation in festivity and ritual and the role of traditional liturgy in a modern/post-modern world. Here, as in many branches of the study of Christian liturgy and ritual, one can speak of a dynamic interplay of cultus and culture which leads to a creative interaction between new questions, new sources, and new techniques and research methods.[1]

II. Pilgrimages and pilgrim accounts

The old pilgrimage routes in Europe are busy these days: thousands upon thousands of usually individual and non-affiliated pilgrims spend weeks, even months, on the way towards the traditional goals of pilgrimage such as Rome, Assisi, Chartres and the Holy Land. The old medieval routes to Santiago de Compostela in Spain are far and away the most popular: from all corners of Europe people walk and cycle to the tomb of St James. However, this European 'pilgrimage boom' also seems to focus on smaller local and regional goals.

Here a number of questions arise. Is there really a renaissance throughout the spectrum of pilgrimage? Should we speak of continuity or discontinuity within the pilgrimage tradition? What is the 'religious content' of pilgrimage, what are its motives, effects and functions? Are people seeking holiness and healing, or is this just one more instance of the omnipresent shift from touristic culture to cultural tourism? Finally, we can look for relevant global cultural processes which can serve as fruitful frameworks of interpretation. What should we be considering in this regard? The return of religion in a modern/post-modern period? Or is this rather a 'culturalization' of religion? How do we interpret this success of tradition?

We now have available an interesting source for the theme of modern pilgrimage. Many pilgrims keep a diary, and thus we possess unique material for research which we have lacked so often in the past: a first-person account which can set us on the trail of the reception and experience of Christian ritual by the participants themselves, the kind of account which is so much sought after.[2]

What answer can we give to the questions asked above on the basis of this specific source?

A wealth of accounts of pilgrimages came out of The Netherlands and Belgium around 1980, after first emerging in the late 1960s. From approximately 100 collected Dutch pilgrimage accounts of various natures and types I have selected 6 for thorough examination (Annink 1980, Santiago de Compostela; Bosch 1986, Assisi; Lamer 1987, Santiago de Compostela; Vuijsje 1990, Santiago de Compostela; Houdijk and Houdijk 1990, Santiago de Compostela; Post 1991, Rome).[3] I shall give only an impression of the analysis and interpretation of other similar publications.[4]

Three levels are to be distinguished in the account:
(a) the daily account of the experiences of the journey;

(b) contemplative pieces framing the daily account or interpolated into it, describing the perception of the journey;

(c) unspoken messages, the level of the ultimate primary function(s) and or meaning(s) of the pilgrimage in the life of the narrator or the group to which the narration is addressed.

The first level is very consistent in all accounts. Like accounts of experience in boarding schools or extended life stories, the pilgrimage brings with it a series of commonplace elements which may be regarded as a sort of 'script'. Each account pays consistent attention to the established daily model: rising, seeking the way, losing the way, encounters, eating and drinking, seeking shelter for the night, sleeping, weather, impressions of the landscape. There is an emphasis on the elements of surprise which contrast with the daily routines of home. By undertaking these journeys, individuals acquire an interest in things that they would never have paused to look at previously. The first person runs through the trivial level as a sort of *Leitmotiv*; the story is as it were carried by a hero who undergoes a development, a growth, sometimes even a conversion. The resultant first-person form underlines this.

To the first linear narrative level is added a series of more representative segments at a second level. Here a fixed series of themes, plots or narrative are also present.

In all of them, in my view, the following content and themes are dominant:

Departure and arrival. It is striking that the arrival is for the most part narrated briefly and summarily. All the emphasis is on the pilgrimage, the journey itself. In some cases the arrival is something of an anticlimax: 'Is that all . . . ?'

Encounters. An important role is attached to encounters *en route*; these are developed in various ways. The anecdote dominates here. In certain respects the account may also be read as a linking together of usually unplanned, diverse encounters along the way: much space is given to reflection on involvement with other people.

The character and occasion of the pilgrimage. Various experiences on the way provide occasions for digressions, as for example reflections on the religious or liturgical quality of the event (as compared to a walking tour, or as compared to the past, especially the Middle Ages). There is also reflection on the occasions, motives and effects of the journey undertaken and how these change during the journey.

Nature. The constant confrontation with nature during the journey is a dominant theme in all accounts. 'Nature' here is broadly construed. It denotes not only experience of the landscape and changing weather conditions, but also discoveries in relation to the pilgrim's own body. We read digressions which above all verbalize the contrast with the bourgeois existence left behind and sometimes lead to discussions of our estrangement from nature, of nature and the attribution of meaning, of milieu and quality of life, coupled with living in harmony with nature. This association with nature is a 'classic' pilgrimage theme. Research shows clearly how important the emotional and religious value of pilgrimage is as an 'outdoor liturgy'. Experience with nature is also an important source of attraction for the smaller local and regional pilgrimages.

The past. This first of all plays a role in the various cultural/touristic digressions: places of interest invite elucidation in the manner of a travel guidebook, and invite stories about origins and development. Then we find associations with the Christian past which has shaped the religious, personal identity, or which has been a more general cultural denominator. Here we meet both personal reminiscence and a general cultural thread. The opposition between involvement and distance, the present journey and the general past historical framework, plays a part here. The past also functions frequently as a means of bringing several of the points mentioned above into better focus – especially motivation, perception and bestowal of meaning.

Three clusters into which the content of the material can be ordered for analysis would seem to be:

(a) ritual, the journey, the essence of being a pilgrim:
(b) meeting and relations;
(c) the past.

These three clusters form overlapping sets ordered under the supportive and binding denominator of 'experience of contrast' and 'self-presentation'. The purpose of the narrated story is to express a disseminated and narrated consciousness, lived through the journey undertaken as a series of contrast-experiences, experiences which are fundamentally different from the experiences that prevailed before the journey. These touch on quality of life and interaction with nature, other people and a personal past which in turn is embedded in a more general past.

III. Involvement with the past – a 'museum culture'

It appears that popular religious rites and symbols are becoming a branch of what could be described as 'museum culture'. If this is true, and the accounts of pilgrims show signs of presenting pilgrimage as yet one more exploration of a museum, are we not on the track of a new post-modern assignation of meaning to a 'traditional' Christian ritual or an appropriation of it in these terms? Perhaps we are not seeing a pilgrimage but rather a cultural, ritual framework for the diverse individual presentations of a range of contrasting experiences.

The development of 'museum culture' involves a certain form of involvement with cultural elements, a certain mapping out of human experiences. Objects are primarily in focus here, but quite certainly rites should also be included, in particular rites of popular religious culture such as pilgrimage. In this process we find a hypothetical diagnosis of time or culture which engages in a double movement: there is a development of historicization, an involvement with the past which among other things tends to regard cultural elements as purely expressions of a strange other life; and one of aestheticization, which transforms everything into the pretty, the beautiful, and in the end reduces it to the mere appearance of beauty. Wolfgang Zacharias pointed to an embodiment of this process in the Cologne prelate who tagged the crucifix on his deathbed with the label 'Poor workmanship, eighteenth century'. He died as he had probably lived, in a museum.[5]

The development of a 'museum culture' therefore chiefly involves experiential change, caused by some loss of experience or reality. The involvement with cultural elements is determined by distance, by viewing, rather than by integration with everyday life.

In my view, in the modern and post-modern pilgrim accounts and indirectly in modern and post-modern pilgrimage the past functions as an evocation of the wholly other; we read of the irreconcilable contrast with the mediaeval pilgrims, who are fascinating precisely because they are inaccessible and other. The journey which is undertaken is in important ways seen as a journey into the past. There is a search for a way to summon the experiential world of the past, a desire to link the past with direct experience. This is all summarized in the constantly recurring formula 'becoming a Christian'.

The way in which experiences are related in modern and post-modern pilgrim accounts in so far as they are concerned with the past, strikes me as evidence that they are involved to a very high degree indeed in the process of the development of a museum culture. As we have seen, many experiences are viewed in the light of the everyday life that those on the journey have left behind for varying lengths of time. This is something which stands in the much broader context of the functions of popular religious rituals in the past and today. The pilgrims appear to be wrestling with a constant sense of contextual and functional change. In part I would like to interpret their accounts as an unmistakable sign of the transformation of popular religious and liturgical culture into a museum culture. An old ritual is performed in the 1980s and 1990s, but performed in a new context. Because of the shift in context, the resultant experiences constantly become confusing.

The involvement with the past displayed by pilgrims in our day and the shifts in context and function which I have indicated can lead us to see pilgrimage in the context of 'museum culture'; we can see the pilgrim as an actor in a performed reality, and make the pilgrim's journey a piece of religious theatre. None of the accounts I know locate themselves in this kind of context; all seek to root the traditional ritual in daily life and experience, the way in which they do this in many ways has the character of a struggle, but also that of a legitimation. The ritual, religious, liturgical component is thus frequently designated as a cultural component.

We should, though, be aware that by their relationship with the traditional aspects of the pilgrimage, pilgrims find themselves on the borders of theatre. One of the Santiago accounts, that by Herman Vuijsje, refers directly to the consequences of a complete change in context and function by an anecdote:

> Somewhere along the route, one of my hosts enthusiastically told me about a group of true pilgrims who had recently passed by: twenty Frenchmen, all in classic pilgrim costumes, with staffs and gourds. There were several doctors among them, and also journalists and a television producer. Their luggage was in a chauffeur-driven car. Here we find the ultimate consequences of all the developments which threaten the authenticity of the *Camino*. Pilgrims as actors in a hyper-reality, an enacted reality. The *Camino* as an artificial evocation of something that in fact it no longer is . . . It's only a question of time before turnstiles are installed, a life-sized image of the apostle is mounted on the gable of the cloister, and after every mass well-meant applause will be heard.[6]

IV. A new pilgrim?

Questions about involvement with the past are essentially contained within the question of tradition and modernity/post-modernity; they are questions about the degree of change or continuity in the pilgrimage ritual, tradition or fashion, changes in function or motives. Pilgrimage, above all pilgrimage to Santiago, is seen as an interesting old tradition which people wish to take up. But while the question is one of continuity and tradition, there is also discontinuity. Perhaps it is their concern with the old tradition that differentiates these pilgrims from other pilgrims. In motive and function, present-day pilgrimages along old traditional paths towards old cultural historical regions, deeply rooted in Europe's history, are fundamentally different from traditional pilgrimages. Or perhaps, rather, it is not the pilgrimages but the pilgrims themselves who are so different. A single type of pilgrimage can be appropriated by different people in completely divergent ways. The accounts by pilgrims constantly show how important this appropriation is felt to be. The past is used, invoked and deployed as a kind of vessel which can be filled depending on individual necessities, a ritual framework offered by the possibilities of contrasting experience which pilgrims can fill individually according to their own insights and most of all their own needs.

Every ritual fulfils this role to some extent and serves as a vessel, but pilgrimage provides to a high degree an open framework, and its structure itself determines the degree of attraction and the function to a very important extent.

So I would in no sense want to associate the renaissance of this sort of pilgrim account solely with various reflections on altered pilgrim behaviour, the return to religion or the incurable religiosity of humanity. Pilgrimage attracts because it is 'traditional'. Various compensating functions play an unmistakably important role here: the past, a traditional ritual such as pilgrimage, offers a firm footing in a modern, hectic and above all minimally surprising or exciting existence; it also offers support for an existence in which identity and interpersonal relations have diminished, run amok or become confused. This firm footing is sought as a means of orientation on the future. The quest can possess a clear religious component, but need not.

This very important factor of the past, of tradition, brings us to the differences from other pilgrimages. A completely new type of pilgrim and pilgrimage is emerging: as well as the concern with continuity and tradition which has already been noted, innovation is also involved, in the sense of a function or appropriation which is different in principle. Here we may rightly speak of the 'success of the traditional', but there is also a fundamental shift in signification and adaptation: these are less explicitly religious, and do not completely cover the contrasting experiences which others sketched with themes such as community and solidarity. Of the complex system of actions which comprise pilgrimage, in the cases we are now considering only the vague cultural contours of a generally applicable vessel or ritual remain. Through a detour to the past, pilgrims seek identity and quality of life by means of a series of contrasts in experiences. As in so many other places in the modern world, tradition here offers an island of time and meaning. I also see traditional goals such as Lourdes, and many other forms of the traditional Christian repertoire, as being increasingly taken over in this manner.

Notes

1. See the long-standing multi-disciplinary Dutch research programme on Christian pilgrimage since 1986, and since 1995 the research programme of the Liturgical Institute of Tilburg, *Liturgische bewegingen en feestcultuur. Landelijk Onderzoekprogramma Liturgiewetenschap*, 1995.
2. See the accounts of pilgrimages to Santiago mentioned in the bibliography below.
3. The years refer to the publication of the account, not the pilgrimage itself.
4. For the details of the corpus accounts, method and analysis see P. Post, 'Pelgrimsverslagen: verkenning van een genre', *Jaarboek voor Liturgie-onderzoek* 8, 1992, 285–331; id., 'Pelgrims tussen traditie en moderniteit. Een verkenning van hedendaagse pelgrimsverslagen', and, 'Thema's, theorieën en trends in bedevaartonderzoek', both in J. Pieper, P. Post and M. van Uden (eds.), *Bedevaart en pelgrimage*, Baarn 1994, 7–37 and 253–301 respectively; id., 'The Modern Pilgrim. A Study of Contemporary Pilgrim's Accounts', *Ethnologia Europaea 24*, 1994 [1995], 85–100.
5. See W. Zacharias (ed.), *Zeitphänomen Musealisierung: Das Verschwinden der Gegenwart und die Konstruktion der Erinnerung*, Essen 1990, 29, referring to B. Waldenfels, *Stachel des Fremden*, Frankfurt 1990.
6. H. Vujsje, *Pelgrim zonder god*, Amsterdam 1990, 121.

Select Bibliography

Pilgrims' Accounts

Aebli, H., 1991, *Santiago, Santiago . . . , Auf dem Jakobsweg zu Fuss durch Frankreich und Spanien. Ein Bericht*, Stuttgart (fourth ed.).
Annink, H., 1980, *Een late pelgrim op de melkweg. Een retourtje Enschede-Santiago de Compostela. 5500 kilometer te voet*, Den Haag.
Bentley, J., 1992, *The Way of Saint James. A Pilgrimage to Santiago de Compostela*, London.
Bosch, L., 1986, *Pelgrimeren naar de vrede. Pelgrimstocht naar Assisi, 7 Juni-24 August*, Utrecht (privately published).
Fiennes, J., 1991, *On Pilgrimage. A Time to Seek*, London.
Hanbury-Tenison, R., 1991, *Spanish Pilgrimage*, London.
Houdijk, C. and Houdijk, J., 1990, *Naar de ware Jacob: dagboek van een voerttocht naar Santiago de Compostela*, Schoorl 1990.

Lamers, H., 1987, *Dagboek van een pelgrim naar Santiago de Compostela*, Utrecht (privately published).
Neilands, R., 1985, *The Road to Compostela: Discovering the Pilgrim's Road*, Ashbourne.
Post, H., 1991, *Te voet naar Rome. In het spoor van Bertus Aafjes*, Schoorl.
Buijsje, H., 1990, *Pelgrim zonder god*, Amsterdam.

Select bibliography

Boissevain, J. (ed.), 1992, *Revitalizing European Rituals*, London.
Dupront, A., 1987, *Du sacré. Croisades et pélérinages, images et langages*, Paris.
Post, J. P. and M. van Uden, (eds.), 1994, *Bedevaart en pelgrimage. Tussen traditie en moderniteit*, Baarn.
Post, J. P. and J. Pieper, 1992, *De palmzondagviering: een landelijke verkenning*, Kampen.
Scharfe, M., M. Schmolze and G. Schubert (eds.), 1985, *Wallfahrt – Tradition und Mode. Empirische Untersuchungen zur Aktualität von Volksfrömmigkeit*.

I · Anthropology, History, Tradition

Those Who Go on a Sacred Journey: The Shapes and Diversity of Pilgrimages

David Carrasco

The experience and expression of going on a sacred journey has accompanied the formation and renewal of social order throughout human history and in all parts of the globe. The human need to leave home, travel to a sacred place in order to establish ties with sacred beings, gain physical and spiritual healing, and receive new knowledge so that life can be renewed is a fundamental dimension of religious life. Pilgrimage to sacred sites (places of apparitions, birthplaces, tombs, caves, mountains, relic sites), though sometimes carried out in opposition to theological and ecclesiastical authority, is a persistent manifestation of all religions throughout history. This pilgrimage nature of human life is reflected in the Tibetan word for a living creature, human as well as non-human, i.e. *'groba'*, meaning 'one who goes'.[1]

A remarkable diversity of purposes and causes, images and symbols, routes and terrains, miracles and cures, messages and promises, characterize the career of *homo mobilius* which I shall survey in this article. On the one hand there are classical, prototypical pilgrimage traditions such as the great pilgrimages to Jerusalem, Israel (Jewish, Christian and Muslim); Rome, Italy (Christian); Mecca, Saudi Arabia (Muslim); Jeiron, Israel (Jewish); Ise, Japan (Shinto); or Mount Wu-t'ai, China (Buddhist). On the other hand there are hundreds of thousands of other local and regional pilgrimage sites found all over the world and spread throughout religious traditions.

Yet, there appears to be an underlying pattern, a general morphology of experience and expression which links these diverse pilgrimage traditions together. Faced with the multiplicity of pilgrimages, it is useful to think of pilgrimage as involving three developmental stages (separation from the *status quo*, passage through a threshold, and regeneration and a return to social responsibility) leading to social and spiritual renewal. In what follows we will explore: 1. the morphology of pilgrimages and 2. the diversity of pilgrimages with reference to impressive examples from various world religions. In this way, we will see how diversity and similarity constitute and enrich the human quest to gain access to the sacred sources of life and spiritual regeneration.

I. The pilgrimage process

One of the most fruitful studies of pilgrimage processes was done by the anthropologist Victor Turner, whose work on African, Mexican, Muslim, Christian and other pilgrimage traditions reveals a number of shared characteristics in spite of the many differences. The widespread data of pilgrimages show that almost all of them conform in some way to three related stages of 1. separation from a spatial, social and psychological *status quo* and the passage into 2. a marginal or liminal space and set of social relations within which a theophany takes place resulting in a profound sense of community which usually leads the pilgrim 3. to re-enter society as a changed, renewed human being. Drawing on the earlier studies of the Belgian ethnographer Arnold van Gennep, Turner focused his attention on the second stage of rites of passage – the stage of liminality or the character of being or dwelling for extended periods of time in a spatial, social and spiritual *threshold*, as pilgrims often do. In his article 'Pilgrimages as Social Processes' he writes,

> A limen is, of course, literally a 'threshold'. A pilgrimage centre, from the standpoint of the believing actor, also represents a threshold, a place and moment 'in and out of time', and such an actor – as the evidence of many pilgrims of many religions attests – hopes to have there direct experience of the sacred, invisible or supernatural order, either in the material aspect of miraculous healing or in the immaterial aspect of inward transformation of spirit or personality.[2]

Turner discovered that a potent and distinctive form of social community which he called *communitas* emerges in the liminal stages of pilgrimages. *Communitas* means relationships among people, 'jointly undergoing ritual transition' through which they experience an intense sense of intimacy and equality, an 'I-Thou' awareness. '*Communitas* is spontaneous, immediate, concrete . . . undifferentiated, egalitarian, direct, non-rational . . . '[3] In the process of liminality, the pilgrims progressively achieve a release from conformity to general norms and may experience a profound and collective sentiment for humanity which includes or is stimulated by the quest and presence of a sacred space, god and spirit. We will explore the different modes of *communitas* later in this essay. For now, let us focus on the stage of separation in pilgrimages and the experience of liminality.

The process of separation

In general people who undertake a pilgrimage decide to separate themselves from the social and spiritual *status quo*. They may be driven by pain, fatigue, hope, or countless other motives. This geographical and social separation is often symbolized by the taking of a vow, the making of a promise (*promesa*), or the affirmation of an obligation to leave home and travel to a holy place. Whether the separation from home, social status and daily routine is voluntary or obligatory, a *break* with the social and spiritual *status quo* is completely necessary. This separation may be symbolized in many ways such as through the taking of a new name, the discarding of the usual wardrobe, the writing of one's last will and testament, the cutting of one's hair, or the speaking of a new language. The crucial point is that the pilgrimage begins by one being *set apart*.

Another way that the theme of *separation* is built into pilgrimages is in the location of many, though not all pilgrimage sites, outside the centres of towns and cities. That is, the pilgrimage centre is separated from the political and social centre of culture. This is especially true in central Mexico, where the great pilgrimage centres of the Virgin of Guadalupe at Tepeyac which attracts pilgrims from all over the world, of Our Lady of Zapopan near Guadalajara which attracts pilgrims from many areas in Mexico, and of Our Lady of Ocotlan in Tlaxcala, are all located (or were originally located) on the outskirts of the populated areas of cities and towns.[4] A similar pattern of separating many pilgrimage sites from the centres of towns can be found in the most popular contemporary European Catholic traditions, including shrines at Lourdes, Fatima Czenstoshowa, La Salette and Oostacker. And as we shall see, many pilgrimage traditions lead people to shrines and temples in mountains and other landscapes covering hundreds of miles through and beyond urban settings.

Liminality and communitas

Once pilgrims have made their vow, promise and symbolic and geographical separation, they enter into the experience of *flow*, change, exposure to new landscapes, food and eating habits, ideas, strangers, dangers and uncertainties. The world becomes a bigger place with hardships, novelties and a marvellous potential for comradeship. As Turner notes, the liminal passage of the pilgrim enhances opportunities of human bonding and also bonding with sacred forces. A prime example of *liminal flow* appears in the Hindu tradition of entering sacred *ksetras* (areas), which include forests, groves or mountain regions. These spaces, through which pilgrimages pass, are inhabited by deities who hunt, fight and play games with one another. 'Pilgrimage through *ksetras* is tantamount to participating in the holy experience itself.'[5] One enters into and bonds with the spaces, actions and adventures of the gods.

Turner calls this bonding *communitas*, and describes three kinds of *communitas* which can appear in pilgrimages. The first type is *existential*, or *spontaneous communitas*. This is the unplanned, intensive, direct and total confrontation of human identities involved in the pilgrimage. Moments of spontaneous *communitas* are like 'happenings' rather than pre-ordained rituals, and result in a momentary sense of profound freedom from social norms and biases and a new sense of collective identity. Pilgrims encountering the music or the silences of pilgrimages, the experience of equal status, the fatique and perhaps dangers of the journey, may undergo this kind of *communitas*. Spontaneous *communitas* often contributes to a desire for somewhat more organized repetitions and *normative communitas*, the second type of *communitas* is developed. While spontaneous events of bonding, community and religious experiences take place on pilgrimages, they are characterized mainly by normative *communitas*. Normative *communitas* means the organizing of resources (transportation, food, lodging, liturgy) to keep the pilgrims moving, thriving, communicating with a sense of collective goals in mind. The pilgrimage must be mapped according to the tradition, participants must follow requirements of preparation, the caravan must be organized, clerics or guides must advertise and choose the pilgrims, hospices must be established along the route, teachers must be provided to insure proper education and time must be set aside for crucial moments of illumination, the telling of vows, prayer and the local circumambulation of the shrines. This sense of ordered movement is reflected in the Tibetan term for pilgrimage, *gnas-skor*, meaning the 'circumambulation of sacred places', the following of a prescribed sacred circuit. As one nears the holy place, these normative guides open the pilgrim to a direct sense of the spiritual force of the site and a profound awareness of sharing the experience with fellow pilgrims.

One of the most powerful aspects of pilgrimages is the expression of symbols and images of the new sense of community between human beings and between human beings and their gods. Turner calls this *ideological communitas*, meaning the 'utopian models or blueprints of societies believed by their authors to exemplify or supply the optimal conditions for existential *communitas'*. Ideological *communitas* may appear in scripture, poetry, manifestos, paintings, or even large architectural assemblages expressing ideal-type images of new social and spiritual relationships. Examples include the many images of the Virgin Mary which offer healing, forgiveness and love to the faithful. A prime example is the sacred image of the Virgin of Guadalupe in Mexico, which has been reproduced millions of times and, like a pilgrim, circulates in cars, buses, even as tattoos, around Mexico City, Latin America and the world. In the Buddhist tradition we see ideological *communitas* expressed in the image of Avalokitesvara, a bodhisattva of universal compassion whose visage appears in paintings (with eleven heads representing the all-seeing lord), and sculptures spread far and wide for pilgrims to visit and see.[6]

In specifically religious pilgrimages, the pilgrims move towards the *sacred* source of *communitas*, in space or in the imagination. This allows the pilgrim eventually to return home and face the routines and rigours of life with a new sense of purpose and hope.

II. The diversity of pilgrimage: examples from world religions

'My pilgrimage broadened my scope. It blessed me with a new insight'
(Malcolm X on his pilgrimage to Mecca)[7]

Sometimes the life of a single individual is radically changed and often a profound sense of human and social solidarity is experienced by the group of pilgrims. The result can be a new psychology, a new world view and an enlarged sense of who populates one's social and spiritual community.

One of the most influential and significant pilgrimages taken by a single individual in recent years, revealing their diversity, morphology and power, was undertaken by Malcolm X, whose name was changed to El-Hajj Malik El-Shabazz and whose racial world view was radically transformed. Within the account of his pilgrimage we catch a glimpse of human and cultural diversity within a pilgrimage tradition.

Malcolm X, whose given name was Malcolm Little, had already undergone a profound change of identity and world-view during his years in prison when the Nation of Islam had turned him away from the life of a thief and a convict into Minister Malcolm X, the second most influential Black Muslim in the United States. He internalized the focused, powerful, but provincial and racist world view of the Nation of Islam until he began to break with Elijah Muhammad, the group's sacred leader. During this period of crisis, Minister Malcolm undertook the 'Hajj', one of the five Pillars of Islam, the basic devotional duties of Muslim religion. One scholar of Islam describes the Hajj this way.

> The Hajj permits the worshipper to travel in body to the sacred centre (the shrine in Mecca) where Muslims believe that Adam and Eve lived, where Abraham and his son Ishmael erected the Ka'ba as the first house of worship of the One True God, and where Muhammad often raised up the Salat (the obligatory Muslim prayer service, held five times daily) and led his fellow believers, even when they were persecuted cruelly as they prostrated in prayer and praise.[8]

In fact, over three million Muslims take the Hajj to Mecca each year and follow a complex series of pilgrimage paths in and between the cities of Mecca and Medina. There are specific gates, entrances, movements, visitations and prayers which must be followed by the pulsating mass of pilgrims. There are Hajj manuals and a Hajj industry of services for pilgrims from around the world which help guide the pilgrims to the site sometimes called 'the place where men pray together'.

Malcolm X joined the millions of pilgrims who travelled to Mecca in 1964. His description of his experience gives us a sense of both the communitas, i.e. the diversity of Muslim pilgrimage, and the powerful social and spiritual experience of oneness that one may undergo. In answer to a question about what had impressed him the most about the Hajj, he wrote,

> The brotherhood! The people of all races, colours, from all over the world coming together as one! It has proved to me the power of the One God . . . I have been utterly speechless and spellbound by the graciousness I see displayed all around me by people of all colours . . . There were tens of thousands of pilgrims, from all over the world. They were of all colours, from blue-eyed blonds to black-skinned Africans . . . On this pilgrimage, what I have seen, and experienced, has forced me to re-arrange much of my thought-patterns previously

held, and *to toss* aside some of my previous conclusions . . . And in the *words* and in the *actions* and in the *deeds* of the 'white' Muslims, I felt the same sincerity that I felt among the black African Muslims of Nigeria, Sudan, and Ghana.[9]

There is an endless number of pilgrimages which illustrate different kinds of *communitas* and new psychology. Some outstanding examples which show us the range of pilgrimage traditions include Hindu pilgrimages to Banaras, Catholic pilgrimages to Compostela, and external and internal pilgrimages in Asia.

III. Pilgrimage, sacred sight-seeing and death overcome

A pilgrimage which is largely though not exclusively national takes place at the city of Banaras, or Kashi, in India. Hindus from all over India orientate their minds, imaginations, and even their deaths toward the City of Light, where the Buddha gave his first sermon under the Bodhi tree after he achieved nirvana. When Hindus go on a pilgrimage to or within Banaras they call it '*darshana*' or seeing. These pilgrims are not 'sight-seeing', but they are '*sacred sight-seeing*'.[10] They go to see the sacred city, its thousands of sacred sites, and especially to gaze into the faces of the gods. Central to pilgrimage in India and to Banaras is the concept of *tirtha-yatra*, or tours to the *tirthas* – sacred fords or crossing places. Pilgrims go to Banaras because it is *the* cosmic *tirtha*, or crossing place. For Hindus, the rigorous journey sharpens and deepens their ability to see the gods. They walk long distances weighed down by bundles or travel in overcrowded trains and buses.[11]

Banaras is a particularly interesting pilgrimage centre because the cosmic directions, the peripheral gods as well as pilgrims, travel to Banaras. Some call it the city of all India. This means in part, that all the *tirthas*, or sacred crossing-points to the gods, which in fact are distributed throughout India, are considered magically also to be located within the city. In this way the city is the microcosm of the entire Indian continent and Hindu cosmology. Not only have all the *tirthas* come to Banaras, but the seven sacred cities distributed throughout the country are also considered to be contained within the boundaries of the cultural capital.

Banaras has many names, including Kashim, 'City of Lights', Avimukta, 'The Never-Forsaken', Anandavana, 'The Forest of Bliss', Rudravasa, 'The City of Shiva', and Mahashmashana, 'The Great

Cremation Ground'. In this last name, we see the greatest attraction the city has for pilgrims. As the great cremation ground, the city is the most auspicious of places to die, because it is also the paramount crossing place to liberation. Some pilgrims come to Banaras in order to die and be cremated in the holiest place on earth. As one scholar summarizes it, 'For death in Kashi is death transformed. As the saying goes, *"Kashyam maranam muktih"* (Death in Kashi is liberation). It is dying that unleashes the greatest holy power of Kashi, the power of bestowing liberation, *Moksha* or *mukti*.'[12]

IV. Periphery and centre: pilgrimage bones at Compostela, Spain

The Catholic pilgrimage tradition to Santiago de Compostela in Spain enlarges our awareness of the similarities and differences in pilgrimages. Over the centuries, the favourite sites for international Christian pilgrimages have included Jerusalem, where Jesus had walked, and Rome, where Peter and Paul had died as martyrs – two cities which served as majestic *centres* of religious experience and orientation. During the course of Christian history, pilgrimage centres also appeared in *peripheral* communities (towns which on the surface seemed destined to be places of little account) wherever Christians lived and worshipped. One such site was Compostela, where a legend describes a miraculous discovery that transformed the periphery into a vital centre of pilgrimage and faith.

A hermit named Pelayo and other people saw strange starlight and heard angelic voices near a wooded area and went to investigate. Convinced that something of extraordinary importance was beckoning people to the woods, Pelayo went to the bishop, Theodomir, with the news. The bishop fasted for three days, searched the thick woods, and discovered a hut containing a marble coffin. Inside they discovered the bones of Saint James and a parchment with the full description of how the bones had arrived in Spain. The king, convinced that Pelayo and the bishop had found the remains of one of the apostles of Christ, built the church which eventually became the cathedral of Compostela, a name derived from *campus stellae*, or 'field of the star'.

The site's religious power, due in part to its association with a relic, increased from the twelfth century on, and today Compostela is one of the most popular pilgrimage sites in Christendom. This story of its origin shows how peripheral places and marginal people sometimes play crucial roles in the religious events that found a pilgrimage site. In this way, pilgrimage sites are places of *inclusion* and not primarily places of exclusion. As is often the case, a person of humble origin receives a sign, message or illumination while travelling or away from the centre of town. This peripheral location parallels the marginal social status of the person. But the marginal person is the messenger that God has chosen to communicate his will to the faithful. Then, this outsider shares the epiphany with a church authority who initially resists the message but then is convinced that a new revelation is at hand. Once convinced, the authorities claim the location for the church and a shrine is built on the spot. In time, it becomes a building or site of *monumental importance* and pilgrims travel to the location in search of a miraculous illumination or healing.[13]

V. Mountains and souls: external and internal pilgrimages in Asia

Thus far we have focussed on pilgrimages to cities and local, peripheral centres. In Asian religions we are confronted in abundance with two other types of pilgrimages – pilgrimages to sacred mountains and internal pilgrimages. The internal pilgrimage and its relation to the journey across the landscape, while found everywhere, is perhaps most evident in the Buddhist pilgrimage traditions of China, Tibet and Japan.

Pilgrimages to sacred mountain sites have been popular in China and Japan for millennia. Buddhists, Shinto and Confucian pilgrims travel to sacred mountains where shrines to gods and goddesses, ancestors, spirits and the many Buddhas are found. For instance, the topography of Japanese pilgrimages is impressive in variation and distance. Throughout China and Japan, the mountains are holy places which attract the strenuous efforts of pilgrims to climb and worship. From the eighth to the twelfth centuries in Japan, members of the imperial families, the nobility and Buddhist monks made pilgrimages to remote holy mountains including Mt Kumano, Mt Koya and Mt Kinpu. In the following centuries, pilgrimages were undertaken by the populace at large, and even though governments restricted travel between provinces, pilgrimages were allowed to traverse boundaries.

Among the most impressive pilgrimages in Japan are the pilgrimages to either one particular holy place or to a complex set of sites. In the first case are the pilgrimages to the illustrious Ise, one of the most important Shinto shrines, as well as to individual sites on holy mountains.

Outstanding pilgrimage networks include the Pilgrimage to the Thirty-Three Holy Places of Kannon, a female *bosatsu*, or bodhisattva, whose compassion is unlimited and all embracing. One of the most extensive pilgrimage traditions in Japan is the Pilgrimage to the Eighty-Eight Temples on the Island of Shikoku, which covers a route of 746 miles. Pilgrims must visit the eighty-eight temples according to a prescribed order. This pilgrimage network involves complex relationships between the populace at large and the temple communities which maintain the temples and minister to the pilgrims.

One of the most impressive aspects of Buddhist pilgrimages is the homology between the external pilgrimage to find the Buddha in the world and the meditative pilgrimage to discover the Buddha nature within oneself. (Analogous patterns of joining the search for the soul and the outer pilgrimage appear in Christianity, Judaism, Islam and many other traditions.) The inner pilgrimage can be carried out in the sacred confines of a monastery, where the initiate is required to chant, pray, concentrate and visualize the cosmos, one's own pilgrimage through it, and to nurture the 'Buddha nature' within one's self. Central to this inner pilgrimage is the *mandala*, a Sanskrit word meaning 'circle'. Also used in Hinduism and Tibetan Lamaism, mandalas are laid out in the form of a geometric diagram with numerous variants but always with a centre, an axis and directional headings. The mandala as a central piece in a pilgrimage of inner liberation consists of an assemblage of deities arranged in hierarchical order around a central divinity. The novice who seeks true knowledge of the cosmos, one's own nature and the nature of the Buddha must concentrate, focus, be silent, chant, and visualize the inner nature of the images which make the mandala. The goal of the person meditating on the deities and their forces is to follow a prescribed route and arrive at the centre of the mandala, the centre of truth, and unite with the central deity. 'Through his intense meditation, the officiant realizes the universe being represented, animates the deities and their forces, and unites himself with the central divinity.'[14] This inner pilgrimage may take months or years, depending on the tradition and stage of one's awareness.

In this article I have described pilgrimages through attention to a shared morphology and diverse manifestations in different religious traditions. We see that pilgrimages are both individual and collective experiences, undertaken to renew the pilgrim's life and relation to society and the gods. I believe that all pilgrimages are also in some sense a combination of the outer and inner journey. The search for an experience of wholeness in terms of our outer and inner lives may be the shared goal of all pilgrims on this earth.

Notes

1. Edwin Bernbaum, 'Pilgrimage: Tibetan Pilgrimage', *The Encyclopedia of Religion*, ed. Mircea Eliade, New York 1987, Vol. 11, 351–3: 351.

2. Victor Turner, *Dramas, Fields and Metaphors: Symbolic Action in Human Society*, Ithaca 1974, 196–7.

3. Ibid., 274.

4. Ibid., 193.

5. Surinder M. Bhawdwaj, 'Pilgrimage: Hindu Pilgrimage', *The Encyclopedia of Religion* (n. 1), Vol. 11, 353–4: 353.

6. One obvious example of ideological *communitas* comes from the famous March on Washington, DC, in 1963, when Martin Luther King, Jr, speaking to hundreds of thousands of people who had travelled there, gave his 'I Have a Dream' speech. In the speech, King described the awful centuries of slavery and struggle of African Americans (a painful social pilgrimage through history) and pronounced his utopia of all peoples in America, 'sitting down together at the table of brotherhood'. In this case, King merged the Christian image of *communitas* with Jesus, the sacred meal, with the American ideology of freedom and justice for all to create a modern moment of spontaneous *communitas* for civil rights pilgrims!

7. Malcolm X, *The Autobiography of Malcolm X*, with the assistance of Alex Haley, New York 1973, 317.

8. Frederick M. Denny, *Islam and the Muslim Community*, San Francisco 1987, 53.

9. Malcolm X, *Autobiography* (n. 7), 388–92.

10. Diana Eck, *Banaras, City of Light*, Princeton 1983, 12.

11. All pilgrims to Kashi follow the path of the 'sadhus' or the 'sannyasins' – the holy men or the renouncers whose lifelong devotions to spiritual truth provide the model for sacred sight-seeing. In fact, for these specialists, wandering itself is a form of salvation. One Hindu text, the *Aitareya Brahmana*, has the god Indra, the protector of travellers, tell a young man, 'The feet of the wanderer are like the flower, his soul is growing and reaping the fruit. And all his sins are destroyed by his fatigues in wandering. Therefore, wander' (ibid., 21).

12. The attraction of Banaras for the human pilgrims is partly due to the fact that the Eight Directions of the Universe originated there and spread out across the universe, organizing it and providing ways for pilgrims to come to the centre of the world (ibid., 325).

13. It is important to note that there have also been thousands of small churches throughout Catholic Europe which serve as local pilgrimage centres, coming to life at least once a year on the feast day associated with a saint or relic. As other articles in this issue show, another major type of pilgrimage centre in Christianity is that dedicated to the worship of the Virgin Mary, either in the form of a miraculous statue or sanctified by an apparition of the Virgin and the transmission of a message

to a believer. Today, for instance, over three million pilgrims travel to Lourdes each year.

14. E. Dale Saunders, 'Mandalas: Buddhist Mandalas', *The Encyclopedia of Religion* (n. 1), Vol. 9, 155–8: 156.

Jesus the Pilgrim

Sean Freyne

The idea of Jesus as pilgrim suggests interesting historical and theological questions, but it also provides a focus for our personal and communal journeys at this particular juncture in history. Contemporary trends in philosophy, the social sciences, literature and even the natural sciences have all made us more keenly aware of the transitory nature of our universe and our lives. However, the notion of change can easily spill over into that of the impermanence and provisionality of existence itself. Thus the journey motif has experienced a timely resurgence as an evocative symbol in our own day for the spiritual quest. In addition to the image of the spiritual journey of those in search of God, there is also the understanding of God's self as the God of the exodus rather than the abstract God of classical theism, based on the Greek philosophical speculation about unchanging essence.

Pilgrims are not any kind of journey-people, however, since pilgrimage points to a particular centre to which individuals and groups feel drawn. It depends on those two basic dimensions of our existence, time and place, in order to symbolize at once the longing in the human heart and the presence of God in our world. Together they highlight both the human search and the divine self-disclosure that holds out the promise of a permanent and total union. Both aspects are central to all the great world religions, but find particular cultural expressions in different historical religions. Pilgrimage to the central sanctuary in Jerusalem became the hallmark of the Israelite religious experience from the beginning of the Davidic monarchy in the tenth century and was reinforced by the Deuteronomistic reform in the seventh: 'Three *times* a year all your men folk are to appear before Yahweh your God in the *place* he chooses' (Deut. 16.16). These three feasts were Passover, Pentecost and Tabernacles. The origins of the central sanctuary to which all Israel was summoned marked a stage in its political development from tribal confederation to centralized monarchy. This stage also corresponded to the religious development of a strict monotheism as expressed in the *Shema* prayer: 'Hear O Israel, the Lord your God is one' (Deut. 6.4). This reform, important as it was in the context of the threat to Israel's distinctive memory of its God who had called it out of Egypt, had the effect of creating a separation between that God and Israel. A boundary was established which marked off the sacred from the everyday, and the sense of intimacy with Yahweh's moving presence in the desert wanderings was lost. To compensate for this, the theme of exodus became transformed into that of pilgrimage, forming part of a network of symbolic expressions through which Israel sought to maintain its communal and religious identity.

Jesus the pilgrim

To speak of Jesus as pilgrim is to situate him very definitely within his own religious tradition of the regular journey to Jerusalem, the support for the temple there and the celebration of Yahweh's deeds of liberation, all essential elements of the religious experience of the pilgrims. The religious literature of Judaism – psalms, narratives, visionary literature and legal codes – building on the Deuteronomic ideal sees the Jerusalem temple as the symbolic centre of a shared belief system. The threat to that centre made a deep impact. From Babylon there is the poignant song of loss as the exiles pine for Zion and the celebrations that can be performed only there (Ps. 137). Second Isaiah resounds with joyous songs of the returnees as they travel home triumphantly through the desert, echoing the Hallel psalms which the pilgrims sang as they came in sight of Jerusalem on the *aliyah* or ascent to the holy city. Ezekiel's vision of the new temple as the centre of a new creation continued to resonate through subsequent centuries, most notably among the Essenes as expressed in the Temple Scroll from Qumran. After its destruction by the Romans in 70 CE, the temple continued to play a significant role in the imagination of Jews, its holiness stipulations providing the foundations on which the sages constructed the Mishnaic system. The extent to which this work of the second century continued to be preoccupied with details about the temple, its feasts, sacrifices and obligations, despite the fact that there was no possibility of rebuilding it after the failure of the second revolt in 132–135, is quite remarkable.

To speak of Jesus the Jew is to understand his religious and personal life within this complex, symbolic network. For all who shared this Jewish world of belief, whether they came from Babylon, Asia Minor, Egypt, Rome or Galilee, the Jerusalem temple provided a shared focal point. The pilgrimage itself was a difficult and dangerous enterprise. Even for Galileans it involved a three-day journey as well as the disruption of the normal patterns of life in the home and village. Yet, in affirming one's religious and ethnic identity, it was a deeply reassuring experience. Travelling in caravans of kinspeople and neighbours already generated this deep sense of belonging and community that was such a feature of all peasant, pre-industrial societies, especially the Jewish one. For peasants from the countryside there was the strangeness of the urban environment, echoed in the disciples' expression of awe at the magnificence of the buildings in the Temple precincts (Mark 13.2). The feeling of isolation in striving to live the distinctively Jewish way of life in contexts where this could leave one open to derision, if not downright hostility, was more than compensated for by the emotional experience of such occasions.

Not merely were the bonds of kinship reinforced, but local feuds were settled prior to embarking on such adventures (Matt. 5.23f.). Journey's end brought its own compensations, human as well as religious, particularly the sense of belonging to a faith that had universal appeal, as pilgrims from all the known world were present. Little wonder that prophets such as Isaiah and Zechariah saw the pilgrimage to Zion as a symbol of universal salvation for all the nations, something Luke also draws on in his account of the first Christian Pentecost (Acts 2.1–13). As a result of the feelings generated by the great festivals, celebrating the events on which Israel's hopes were based, these occasions were regarded as high-risk times by the Roman administration, since national fervour was often running high. People returned home spiritually refreshed and with a renewed sense of their own group identity, since the pilgrimage was first and foremost a communal experience of Israel and its God.

This very brief sketch of the pilgrimage's impact on the life of the pious Jew makes the attitude of Jesus the pilgrim all the more difficult to comprehend. However one understands his sense of mission and its inspiration, to have the courage to challenge his own tradition as fundamentally as Jesus did called for courage, commitment and a deep sense of trust in God's providential care, no matter how difficult it was to comprehend the outcome. It was not that there was no precedent for challenging the centre even as one participated in its ritual. From his rural background, the prophet Amos had denounced the corruption and exploitation that a central sanctuary afforded its cultic personnel as early as the eighth century BCE. Thirty years after Jesus's death another rural prophet, Jesus, son of Ananias, had issued oracles of doom against Jerusalem, the city and the people, and significantly he was described as being deranged by the priestly aristocrat, Josephus.

The Essenes represented another form of critique than that of these isolated individuals by establishing an alternative community in the desert which they regarded as replacing the existing, illegitimate temple. Whether or not Jesus should be seen as belonging to this latter category of a movement of protest against the temple or as a lone prophetic voice depends somewhat on how one understands the fact that only he suffered the consequences of his protest; his disciples were not pursued by the authorities. What is undoubtedly significant in terms of our theme is the idea that the earthly Jesus through his action in the temple is an instance of the pilgrim subverting the place of pilgrimage. At least that is the way in which the various evangelists see the episode, especially John (2.19f.). But what was the motivation for this challenge? Was it merely an instance of using an important occasion to challenge the centrality of the temple, or were there other deeper issues at stake for Jesus?

The action in the temple has been variously interpreted as a Zealot-style cleansing, a prophetic critique of unjust trading, a symbolic gesture of overthrowing or a concern for proper observance of the rules governing offerings. Each suggestion has its own plausibility, depending on how one views Jesus' ministry as a whole. One thing seems clear, namely that this was not an isolated incident, but should be interpreted in the light of his complete ministry in Galilee and Jerusalem. It was not that Jesus was disrespectful of the temple or what it symbolized, namely, God's presence to and with Israel.

Rather, it was a matter of how and where that presence was to be encountered. In line with Jesus' prophetic understanding, God was now to be found in meals with sinners, who did not have to await the journey to Jerusalem in order to make the sin offering before receiving forgiveness, or among the poor who had no offerings of any significance to bring, even if they could have made the journey, or in the healings, that is the removal of the social stigma from the blind, the sick and the physically disabled, who were denied full participation in the cultic affairs of the nation according to the purity laws that governed the conduct of affairs in the temple. In Jesus' view the restored Israel would not be divided along the hierarchical lines which the ordering of sacred space in the temple regulated, since God was no longer to be conceptualized as separated from people in varying degrees. God had visited the lowly.

It calls for a special quality of heart and mind to be able to challenge the received orthodoxy of one's own tradition, and on the basis of its authority to attempt to re-centre its most basic claim. Yet this is the lonely, dangerous and challenging role that is the lot of the prophet. Prophets can call on no other authority than that of the inner voice in favouring personal experience over received tradition. Self-doubt is part of the agony that prophets must come through, but in doing so they become free to name the experience in terms of God's spirit. Thus they can point to the ultimate fruits of their vision as the legitimation of the claim that the kingdom of God is here rather than there, demands this kind of action rather than that, is realized now rather than later. The ultimate achievement of Jesus the pilgrim rests in his unqualified response to that call and in his unflinching response to its demands. His journey may have gone the pilgrim way to Jerusalem, but his way pointed beyond, to 'the ends of the earth', since in the prophetic vision the temple was 'the city on the hill' that beaconed to the nations that God was visiting the whole earth. God's presence was to be affirmed at the edges of Israel and of life as well as at its centre in Jerusalem.

From the pilgrim Jesus to a pilgrimage christology

Faced with the loss of their leader in the most demeaning circumstances of crucifixion ('Cursed be everyone who hangs on a tree'), the first followers of Jesus were faced with stark alternatives: *either* return to Galilee and to the previous way of life, abandoning the new horizons experienced with Jesus, *or* attempt to make sense of what had happened in the light of God's plan for Israel. The resurrection experience was, of course, the crucial turning point, the effects of which can be seen in terms of the transformed evaluation of Jesus that they undertook, their changed understanding of the symbolic nature of their own group as the restored Israel, and their sharpened awareness of the new tasks that now faced them. From being frightened Galilean pilgrims, attempting to disguise their identity (Mark 14.27), they became open and bold proclaimers of what their new understanding of Jesus signified from the viewpoint of the restoration eschatology of the prophets. For some (the Hebrews) this meant staying in Jerusalem, since those prophecies had indicated that it was there that restoration would occur (Isa. 2.2–4; 28.16f.). Others (the Hellenists) embarked on a mission to the Diaspora and eventually to the Gentiles, once they had addressed to the Jerusalem authorities the challenge to the received understanding of temple and Torah which for them was implied in Jesus' ministry. We can detect real tensions between these two responses to the meaning of Jesus' life in the subsequent literature from the early generations, since each point of view had very different practical implications, yet it is equally clear that the pilgrimage and its associated set of symbols afforded both suitable categories for articulating their perspectives on the idea of the pilgrim people on mission. Here we can only briefly sample some of the ways in which this imagery found expression in the writings that have come down to us.

Strange as it may seem, it is in Paul's writings, especially in his Epistle to the Romans (chs. 9–11), that one sees how the Hebrews' pilgrimage theology expressed itself in the context of the developing Christian mission. Like every other Jew, Paul could never abandon his sentimental attachment to Jerusalem and the promises associated with it. Yet he was faced with the dilemma of the success of his Gentile mission and how their admission might appear to infringe the principle of Jew first, then Gentiles, which was the essence of the prophetic hope. For this reason Paul was most anxious to maintain good relations with the Jerusalem church, even when he differed radically from them on the conditions of Gentiles' admission.

The Christian community at the heart of Judaism represented for Paul the remnant of the restored Israel from which the full flowering of the one church of Jews and Gentiles would emerge. Only then would the mission have been accomplished and the definitive pilgrimage could take place. Thus the pilgrimage theology that maintained strong links with its Jewish roots in Jerusalem but also acknowledged the role of Jesus within the *mysterion* or plan of God for history was capable of being interpreted inclusively, since it was based on an understanding of a God that recognized no limits and therefore included all.

Ironically, it was only when the Jerusalem connection was broken because of the loss of the temple in 70 CE that it was possible to articulate this insight fully and clearly. The author of the Epistle to the Ephesians developed Paul's thought in the light of the new situation in his moving reflection on Christ as reconciler of Jew and Gentile within the one body. With the imagery of the various temple courtyards designated for different people and its ritual of atonement very much in mind, the Paulinist author writes: 'For he (Christ) is the peace between us and has made the two into one and broken down the barrier which was between them . . . making peace through his cross . . . Through him both have access in the one Spirit to the Father' (Eph. 2.13–18). The author goes on to describe the new reality further as a shared citizenship of the one city and as a temple based on the foundation of the apostles and prophets with Christ Jesus as the corner-stone. Thus all together are being constituted into a single house in the Spirit, where God lives.

The pilgrimage theology of the Hellenists, on the other hand, was developed from an experience of hostility from within mainline Judaism. After the martyrdom of Stephen they were driven out of Jerusalem and compelled to develop a theology of opposition within which temple and pilgrimage imagery played a polemical role with regard to rival claims between the church and the synagogue. It is in such writings as the Fourth Gospel and the Epistle to the Hebrews that one sees this strand of early Christian reflection in its most developed state. Yet despite the atmosphere of hostility surrounding such thinking, it is noteworthy that the Jewish roots are clearly maintained and the hopes for the future are expressed accordingly. It is also important to recall that this strand of replacement theology had already been developed among another dissi-dent group, the Essenes, as already noted. In the Greek world it received a powerful boost through the adoption of categories associated with Plato's philosophy, particularly the distinction between imperfect outer ap-pearances and perfect inner realities – the Platonic world of ideas. In Alexandria, a Jewish Platonist, Philo, had already paved the way by interpreting his biblical heritage in this mode, so there were plenty of precedents for Christian Hellenists to approach the Jewish symbolic universe in a similar vein.

The Fourth Gospel's portrayal of Jesus' ministry is dominated by his journeys to Jerusalem for the Jewish feasts. On each occasion, however, the visit ends in polemic as the pilgrim Jesus declares himself the fulfilment of the feast's spiritual meaning, often expressed through symbols such as bread, light and water. Such claims only lead to a confrontation with 'the Jews', the opponents within the text, who perceive them as blasphemous and to be rejected. The irony of the narrative lies in the fact that the places of origin and destiny of Jesus are vital for understanding his true identity. His opponents judge him on the basis of what is known externally about Jesus, the Galilean pilgrim whose place of origin disqualifies him from being the Messiah. The reader, however, is privy from the Prologue to his true role as the Word made flesh, tabernacling in our midst (John 1.14). His real pilgrimage is not to Jerusalem 'in order to show himself to the world', but to where he was before (John 6.52; 7.1–10). This journey reaches its climax in the final prayer of Jesus (ch. 17), which is his spiritual journey to God in anticipation of his death, interpreted as his glorification. The traditional places of worship, Jerusalem and Mount Gerizim, have been transcended for the true worshippers in spirit and in truth; and the special times of worship, the Jewish feasts, have been subsumed into the present hour which is the fulfilment of all the waiting and hopes (John 4.22f.).

The Epistle to the Hebrews, on the other hand, focussed on the ritual of the Day of Atonement, which culminated in the high priest's entry into the Holy of Holies, there to offer sacrifice on behalf of his own sins and the sins of the people. This solemn ritual marked the climax of the pilgrimage, even for those who were not admitted to the inner courtyards of the temple, since the high priest entered in a representative capacity on behalf of all Israel. The author of the epistle sees this elaborate and solemn ritual, enacted once a year, as a type or forerunner of Christ's entry to God, as the everlasting high priest, 'who offered himself once for all' on behalf of the sins of all. The definitive character of Christ's entry to God only highlights the repetitive and inadequate nature of all previous entries into the earthly tabernacle by successive high priests. Just as in the Johannine writings, here too we encounter the contrast between the real world of heavenly realities and the imperfect one of earth.

Christ's priesthood is likened to that of Melchisedek, who was associated with the universal promises to Abraham, rather than with that of Aaron, from whom the existing priesthood took their origins. The 'good things to come' which are the result of Christ's priestly journey to God are hidden, yet available in faith to the believers who hold fast and do not revert to putting their trust in the earthly sanctuary and its outmoded rituals. For this reason they are exhorted to go outside the city, there to encounter Christ, who died outside the walls. Their faith is no longer in what the existing city symbolized, but rather in the one that is to come, to which they are exhorted to approach in the jubilant mood of pilgrims drawing near to God: 'But what you have come to is Mount Zion and the city of the living God, the heavenly Jerusalem where the millions of angels have gathered for the festival, with the whole church in which everyone is a firstborn and a citizen of heaven' (Heb. 12.22f.).

As models of this Christian way, many heroes of the faith are summoned up from the past, each prepared to journey to the unknown rather than to put their trust in the securities of the present. Abraham and Moses are singled out as outstanding examples of this quality of trust in the future. Their faith was grounded in hope in Jesus, who is the anchor that draws securely beyond the veil where he has entered first (Heb. 6.19f.; 11.1f.). For this author faith is a pilgrimage that opens up the way to God in the company of others who share the belief in Jesus the pilgrim priest who is the leader of those destined to enter the heavenly sanctuary.

Conclusion

Pilgrimage, especially as it was practised in the Jewish religious experience, provided a rich vein to be explored by the early Christian writers as they sought to articulate their faith in what God had accomplished in Jesus and the demands of that faith for all who would seek to follow him. The sense of being drawn to the centre for a full and permanent encounter with God, so essential to the pilgrim's aspirations, corresponded to the realized but incomplete nature of Christian existence within the world. The promise of what lay ahead at journey's end enlightened and enlivened the pilgrim's journey on the way. Each partial encounter increased the longing for the final and complete one when the journey would culminate in rest. In the interim, however, it was impossible to stay rooted at the centre; one had to return to the world and to life's struggles, though secure in the promise that God was indeed not just at the centre, but was in fact the centre wherever the journey was leading. So the return could never mean just going back to the mundane as it was before. The experience inevitably meant being changed, and thus the transformation from pilgrim to missionary was a natural one.

The stimulus for the early Christians to draw so heavily on the pilgrimage and associated motifs originated from a number of factors, not least from the fact that many of them had themselves had such an experience, as well as being acquainted with the rich tradition of hope for Israel that was expressed through these images. This literature provided them with a whole range of colourful, evocative and challenging metaphors in which to express their hopes, beliefs and values. The conviction that the resurrection experience gave them, namely that Jesus had indeed been vindicated by God and that his life and death had ultimate meaning for all of human life, etched the memory of his earthly life in its essential details more firmly than ever on their consciousness. Jesus' earthly pilgrimage may have appeared to have ended in disaster, but now they realized that his real journey had a different goal and deeper implications for him and them. As we recapture some of the different nuances to which this combination of factors gave rise within the early Christian community, we do well to recognize that the tensions we have uncovered between the return to Zion traditions and the heavenly journey motif that transcends the particularities of Jewish hopes are tensions that we too experience as Christian pilgrims on the way. Our lives are lived within the horizons of hope for human wholeness and community where we are, and the longing for union with God, the fulfiller of all human hopes. It is good that the texts which the memory of Jesus have provoked maintain the tensions between these two poles of our existence. Part of the pilgrimage we are called to embark on is the journey back and forth between them, the one ensuring that our hopes are grounded in the search for justice and the other reminding us that our restlessness is of God. 'Arise, let us go hence' (John 14.31).

Pilgrimage in the Christian Tradition

Jaime R. Vidal

In the summer of 1970 I and a fellow student from Fordham University spent two months in Mexico at Ivan Illich's Center for Intercultural Documentation. Practically the first place we visited, at my insistence, was the shrine of Guadalupe; although my heritage is not Mexican, Our Lady of Guadalupe has been the patron of my home town since it was founded in 1670. As the rickety old bus we rode approached the shrine, I found myself mumbling pilgrimage psalms under my breath; 'I rejoiced when they said to me, we shall go to the House of the Lord'; 'Her foundations are upon the holy mountain; the Lord loves the gates of Zion above all the tents of Jacob . . . ' But as we got off the bus and approached the basilica, I was jolted out of my mood by a question from my travelling companion: 'What's the point of coming all the way here to pray? Isn't God everywhere? Can't he hear you just as well when you pray in your parish church?'

Ubiquitous God or holy place?

I allow myself to begin with this personal anecdote because between the two of us my friend and I represented two very common attitudes to pilgrimage. My friend's question has been asked by countless Christians throughout the ages, including Jerome and Augustine, Thomas à Kempis and Erasmus, while my attitude has been shared not only by countless simple believers, but by the likes of René Descartes.[1]

Logically, my friend's question is unanswerable. God *is* everywhere, and God can hear us just as well in one place as in any other. And the gospel itself would seem to side with this position; after all, Jesus does tell the Samaritan woman that her question about the proper place for pilgrimage and worship is an irrelevant question; since God is spirit, God is to be worshipped not in Jerusalem or in Gerizim, but in spirit and in truth (John 4.19–24). As Augustine puts it, since God is everywhere, we cannot approach God by moving our feet, but only by moving our hearts.[2]

Psychologically, it's another story, and Christianity, as an incarnational religion, must take such psychological instincts seriously – they are part of the human nature which the Word has taken up. At the psychological level, the logical position has against it the weight of an almost universal human instinct, the instinct to set space aside as sacred (which in turn frees the rest of human space for profane use), and a concomitant instinct to distinguish between space which *we* have set aside for the divine and space which the divine has in some way chosen for itself, and sacralized *motu proprio*. This is the distinction between 'church' and 'shrine'.

A church is a place which is set aside for the prayerful gathering of the assembly of believers; its location is decided by the availability of land, by the convenience of a site for the needs of the community in terms of visibility, approachability, etc. The location of a true shrine, on the other hand, is decided by the sacred person or force that manifests itself there – often enough in a relatively obscure or inconvenient place; a place that the community or its hierarchy would never have thought of choosing. In such a place a door between worlds has been opened, and a ladder has been seen connecting earth and heaven, or the cloud of the divine presence has been seen to rest. Once such a hierophany has been experienced in a given place, and the experience has been accepted by a community, it is inevitable that others will travel to the same place, seeking perhaps a lesser version of the same experience, or feeling that God will in fact listen to their prayers there in a way that God might not in their parish church. This instinct is spontaneous and present in every religion and every age.[3]

A place thus becomes a shrine by the experience within it of the presence of the sacred to an extraordinary degree. But this sense of extraordinary presence may be movable or immovable, depending on whether the extraordinary sense of presence is intrinsically connected to the place itself or is connected to the place only because it contains an ojbect to which the sense of presence is attached. The first type is a shrine because of something that happened on that spot: an event in sacred history (Bethlehem or Jerusalem), an apparition or a miracle (Lourdes, Guadalupe), or a crucial event in the life of a saint (La Verna, where Francis received the stigmata). The attraction of such places is often connected to what Ewart Cousins calls the 'mysticism of the historical event',[4] by which visitors feel mysteriously connected to the event whose locus they are visiting, and to the spiritual forces which the event released.

The second type of shrine is sacred because it contains the body of a saint, or a cult image believed to be miraculous; since such sacred objects can be moved, the shrine itself is only sacred as long as the relics or image remain in it. There can, of course, be a certain amount of overlap between these categories; thus even after the destruction of Thomas Becket's bones Canterbury Cathedral retained its potentiality as a shrine because it contains the place of Becket's martyrdom.[5] In Guadalupe the priests at the hilltop chapel emphasize the spot of the apparition, while the priests at the basilica, in telling the same story, emphasize rather the miraculous image which hangs over its altar.

The basilica at Guadalupe also serves as an example of the transfer of the sacred object to a new location, which as of that point becomes the shrine; in 1976 the seventeenth-century basilica, which was showing insoluble structural problems, was closed down, and the ancient image was solemnly transferred to a new structure a short distance away. In Russia we find the strange case of a museum becoming an unofficial shrine due to the presence of a venerated cult object. The miraculous ikon of the Virgin of Vladimir was removed by the Soviet government from the Kremlin's Church of the Dormition and hung at the Tretyakov Gallery, but so many 'tourists' would suddenly become worshippers when they reached that particular work of art that the museum authorities had to set up a sign forbidding visitors to bow, kneel or cross themselves on that spot – an injunction which was of course completely disregarded.[6]

Such sacred objects can, in fact, even be taken temporarily to other places, either as a matter of tradition, when an image or relic may be processionally taken from its shrine to some other church or town every year on a certain feast, or because of some extraordinary situation of privilege or public emergency. In 1995, for example, important relics of Saint Anthony visited a number of churches outside Italy to celebrate the eighth centenary of his birth, and were received with great popular enthusiasm. In *War and Peace*, Tolstoy gives a moving description of the procession which brought the miraculous ikon of the Virgin of Smolensk to the army before the battle of Borodino.

Some shrines, such as Zapopan in Mexico, even have a 'pilgrim image' which is sent to other places, while the original image never leaves the shrine. (The *Peregrina* of Zapopan – a lovely image in carved ivory brought from the Philippines in colonial times – wears a traveller's hat and *rebozo* instead of the crown worn by the original, sedentary image.) Such visits of a relic or sacred image to a place away from its original shrine usually occasion local pilgrimage to the place being visited, especially by persons who might not be in a position to visit the shrine itself.

Travel to a far-away holy place is often an individual experience; especially if undertaken on foot, it can separate pilgrims from their normal social environment and experiences, and thus produce an experience of liminality – although it also produces an experience of solidarity with strangers: pilgrims who are met on the road or people living along the route who offer shelter, food or encouragement. The narratives of contemporary pilgrims to Compostela bring out both the liminality and the solidarity in very immediate ways: unlike tourists who can send their family a list of the hotels they will be in, so that they can be reached by letter or international telephone if necessary, walking pilgrims are totally isolated and unreachable, and after a week or two they begin to live in a different world, with different ways of measuring distance in relation to time, and with very different ways of relating to strangers. Fellow pilgrims may walk with you for some hours or a few days and then fall back or forge ahead of you, but if you cross their path again you are old friends. A farmer and his wife may let you sleep in their barn and give you breakfast; you will never meet again, but they expect you to remember them when you kneel at the apostle's tomb.[7] Similar experiences of liminality and solidarity are found in the nineteenth-century Russian classic *The Way of a Pilgrim*.[8]

In contrast to this experience we must also look at the experience of the traditional and collective pilgrimage of a town or a confraternity to a relatively nearby shrine on that shrine's festal day. Here the experience is rather of an enhanced solidarity, as the bonds of neighbourhood are solidified and intensified by the shared worship at a numinous site which – while outside the physical limits of the *polis* – from time out of mind has been associated with the community in question. To withhold oneself from such a celebration would be to cut oneself off from the group's collective identity. In Mediterranean culture this phenomenon goes back to pre-classical times, and is still very much alive; one famous example is the festive pilgrimage of Seville's gypsy *barrio* of Triana to the shrine of Our Lady of *el Rocío*, held each year on Pentecost Monday. Many popular songs emphasize the experience of being part of the joyful crowd of *romeros*, and the fact that one goes there *con Triana*; with all Triana. Such celebrations also have a particular attraction for emigrants, who often make a particular effort to return for a visit precisely at the time of their village's yearly pilgrimage.[9]

Early Christian pilgrimage

It is often said that the practice of Christian pilgrimage originates in the Constantinian age, when St Helena discovered what were believed to be the places where Christ was born, crucified and buried, and built basilicas on the spots. It would seem that Helena was able to identify these places precisely because the Emperor Hadrian, when converting Jerusalem into the Roman city of Aelia Capitolina in 135 CE, had not only built a temple to Zeus on the Temple Mount, but also a temple to Venus on the site of Golgotha[10] and a shrine to Adonis over the cave of Bethlehem. These temples made it impossible for Christians or Jews to visit these places, but ironically they also kept their locations from being forgotten. Hadrian's action also would seem to imply that the Christians (whom he would have regarded as a Jewish sect) were already in the habit of visiting these places out of devotion.

From earliest times the graves of the martyrs were also visited collectively on their anniversaries by the local communities, which celebrated the eucharist there. The earliest known testimony of this custom is the letter from the community at Smyrna to the community of Philomelium, describing the martyrdom of its bishop Polycarp, which can be dated between 155 and 160 CE.[11] It would seem that individuals also visited these graves for personal prayer at other times. The graves of the apostles Peter and Paul at Rome were known and venerated by the local community, and by the many Christians who came to the capital of the empire on personal or ecclesiastical business, though there is no reliable evidence that such a trip was undertaken exclusively for the veneration of the apostles before the Constantinian age.[12] By the late second century Gaius of Rome writes to the Phrygian Proclus that if he were to come to the city he could point out to him the monuments (*tropaia*) of the Roman church's founding apostles, one at the Vatican hill and the other at the Ostian Way.[13] Excavations beneath the high altar of St Peter's basilica have revealed a large number of devotional graffiti invoking the apostle's prayers for individuals and their loved ones. Some of these may date from as early as 150.[14]

The conversion of Constantine, however, gave a great impulse to Christian pilgrimages. The emperor himself built lavish basilicas over the graves of Peter and Paul, and after his mother Helena visited Palestine in order to identify the holy places, he had Hadrian's pagan temples torn down and basilicas built over the cave of Bethlehem and over the site of the crucifixion; this last was connected by colonnades to a domed rotunda built over the cave of the Holy Sepulchre, which his engineers turned into a small free-standing chamber by cutting away the hill from around it. By 333, less than ten years after Helena's visit to Jerusalem, an anonymous pilgrim from Bordeaux (at the other end of the empire) produced the first extant description of the holy places, which already shows a tendency to identify the places not only of Golgotha, the Holy Sepulchre, and the cave of the Nativity, but also of many other incidents in the Old and New Testaments.

This tendency is even more noticeable in the *Peregrinatio* of Etheria, a consecrated virgin from Gallaecia in Spain, whose identifications are sometimes rather naive and inaccurate.[15] In this work, which seems to be a letter addressed to the other consecrated women of her city Etheria also gives detailed descriptions of the Jerusalem liturgy, both in its everyday form and as it was celebrated on the great solemnities of the Nativity, the Presentation, and especially Lent, Holy Week and Easter. She tells of the procession from Bethlehem to Jerusalem on the Nativity, and from the Mount of Olives to the city on Palm Sunday, as well as of the emotional vigil held on Holy Thursday night at the Garden of Olives and the individual veneration of the *Lignum Crucis* on Good Friday. (The Easter Vigil, however, is done 'pretty much as we do it at home'.[16]) The influence of returning pilgrims – many of them bishops or influential clergy – soon led to the adoption of many of these liturgical customs in the churches of both East and West, one example being the custom (which Etheria constantly remarks on as unusual) of reading scriptural passages appropriate to the feasts at the eucharist and liturgy of the hours, instead of using *lectio continua*.

Pilgrimage and crusade in the middle ages

The golden age of Christian Palestine ended in 638, when the Caliph Omar entered Jerusalem as a conqueror. Since the Qur'an considers Jesus the greatest prophet next to Muhammad and also speaks very highly of Mary, the new masters of the Holy Land respected the Christian holy places and left them in the hands of their previous guardians. Local Christians were now second-class citizens, burdened with extra taxes, but on the whole were treated fairly, as were pilgrims from the Byzantine Empire and the kingdoms of the West.

By the eleventh century, however, Palestine had been conquered by the Seldjuks, a more fanatical type of Muslim. Returning pilgrims began to tell stories of harassment and oppression, which culminated in 1010 when the authorities had the basilica of the Holy Sepulchre burned to the ground, although the Byzantine emperor soon negotiated permission for a modest rebuilding. Towards the end of the century Pope Urban II preached a holy war for the recovery of the holy places, and in 1099 the Crusaders stormed Jerusalem and set up a Latin kingdom, which was soon followed by Latin patriarchates in Jerusalem and Antioch. For a few decades pilgrims could visit the holy places within Christian territory, although the surrounding Muslim states would often harass them on the roads, so that military orders such as the Templars and the Hospitallers had to be founded for their protection.

The Latin kingdom, however, was an artificial construct; in spite of new crusades the city of Jerusalem fell to Saladin in 1187, and the last bastion of the kingdom fell in 1291. Once again the holy places were under Muslim rule, but were left in the hands of Christians, although under onerous conditions. From this period on dates the uncomfortable and often scandalous division of the principal churches into areas reserved for the different Christian churches, in schism among themselves and jealously guarding their territories against each other's encroachments.[17] Pilgrims from both the East and the West continued to visit the Holy Land, but the pilgrimage became increasingly hazardous and unpleasant – though the perils and hardships were accepted in a penitential spirit, and in spite of all the act of 'worshipping where his feet once stood' (Psalm 131.7, Vulg.) was an extremely moving experience.

Medieval pilgrimage, however, was by no means limited to the Holy Land. In the East Constantinople was a vast storehouse of major relics, which attracted pilgrims from both East and West, until the terrible sack of 1204, when most of the city's treasures were dispersed throughout the West. One of those which remained in the city, the Crown of Thorns, was later sold to St Louis of France by a financially desperate Latin emperor, and was enshrined at the Sainte Chapelle.

In both East and West the tombs of certain saints became major centres of pilgrimage: St Martin and St Denys in France, St Cuthbert and St Thomas of Canterbury in England, St Francis and St Nicholas in Italy, the Fathers of the Caves in Kiev. The bodies of saints whose original shrines were in Muslim held territory were often stolen from the oppressed local Christians and enshrined in Western cities, as was the case with St Nicholas (from Myra to Bari), St Mark (from Alexandria to Venice) and St Isidore of Seville (from Seville to León). Such *pia furta* also happened in Christian-held territories, with no better excuse than the desire to attract the pilgrims to one's own church;[18] since there were many legends about saints impeding the theft of their relics, the very fact of a successful robbery was taken as a sign of the saint's consent.

In the medieval West, however, two great shrines outshone all others: the tombs of Sts Peter and Paul in Rome, and the tomb of St James the Greater in Santiago de Compostela. Pilgrimage to these became so popular as to be comparable to pilgrimage to Jerusalem. The shrines at Rome had a long history of veneration, as we have seen, and this was enhanced by the presence of the Pope, whose role in Western Christian life became ever more important.[19] What was claimed to be the tomb of Saint James was discovered in the extreme north-west of Spain in the ninth century. The beleaguered Christian kingdoms saw this discovery as a sign of divine favour, and stories of James' appearance to turn the tide of battle against overwhelming Muslim odds soon became popular. The great attraction which the shrine acquired for pilgrims from the rest of Europe seems to be connected with the propaganda of the monks of Cluny, who had been introduced to Spain and highly favoured by the Christian kings.

Aside from the tombs of saints (and relics detached from them and sent to other churches), miraculous images, especially of the Mother of God, also attracted pilgrims in the Middle Ages to places such as Montserrat in Catalonia or Le Puy and Rocamadour in France; miraculous icons also attracted veneration in Constantinople, Mount Athos and Russia. This phenomenon would later spread to the point that practically every town would have a Marian shrine in its vicinity, with a local image which focussed the district's piety and attracted pilgrims from the local area or from farther away.

Reformation and Counter-Reformation

Towards the end of the Middle Ages the *Devotio Moderna* was led to criticize pilgrimages by its desire to spiritualize and rationalize the faith. Thomas à Kempis and other spiritual writers stressed interior religion, while Erasmus mocked the abuses of the shrines and the follies and gullibility of pilgrims. Luther himself nailed his 95 Theses to the door of the castle church which housed the Elector of Saxony's enormous collection of relics on the very day when pilgrims were attracted there by their solemn exposition. The spread of the Reformation was marked by the end of pilgrimages and the spoliation of shrines, often accompanied by the destruction of cult images and relics.

The Catholic reaction to the Reformation tended to defend all the aspects of the old faith which the Reformation criticized as idolatrous or superstitious; these were purified of abuses, but then stressed and encouraged. Thus Baroque piety brought a new flowering of pilgrimages and shrines; the Counter-Reformation princes often gave an example by visiting the shrines themselves and rebuilding them lavishly in the new, exuberant style.

Just as the discovery of the New World offered the Catholic Church an opportunity to make up for the lost populations of northern Europe, so also it offered new spaces to be sacralized by shrines and pilgrimage sites. The hermitage of Guadalupe in Tepeyac by Mexico City is already mentioned as a place of frequent miracles by Cortes' old soldier Bernal Díaz del Castillo, and miraculous images of Mary and the Crucified soon attracted pilgrims in every province of Spain's empire. A good number of these, like the *Señor de Chalma* and Guadalupe itself, were enshrined in sacred sites of the native religions, in a policy which had already been used in the conversion of Europe, but which now often arouses suspicions of syncretism.[20]

The great saints of the Counter-Reformation, such as Philip Neri and Francis de Sales, had great veneration for certain shrines, and not only visited them but recommended the practice. Saint Ignatius Loyola in particular began his new life by a pilgrimage to Montserrat, where he kept an all-night vigil and left his sword as a gift to the Virgin; the cave of Manresa where he experienced what would become the *Spiritual Exercises* is at the foot of the holy mountain. He next went on pilgrimage to Jerusalem, where he tried to stay but was dissuaded by the Franciscan superior; when he and his companions made their vows, one of them was that they should go together to the holy places. This vow they were unable to keep because of a war between Venice and the Turks, but the experience of pilgrimage meant so much to him that he decreed that all novices had to make a pilgrimage on foot to some nearby shrine as part of their formation.

Pilgrimage in modern and contemporary Christianity

The Enlightenment was a time of low appreciation for popular religious practices, and pilgrimage was no exception. The educated classes and the governments were on the whole negative, running the gamut from the desire to reform, control and rationalize popular practices to outright mockery and in some cases repression. In both the Western countries and in Russia the common people were hardly touched by these attitudes, except in so far as the rulings of enlightened despots (and enlightened bishops) impinged upon their devotions – which was more the case in the West than in Russia.

The French Revolution, and its extension to the rest of Europe by Napoleon's campaigns, disrupted both the places and the rhythms of popular pilgrimage. While many shrines did not survive the storm, many others were still remembered with affection by the people and were rebuilt or re-occupied by religious communities after 1815. In the East the patterns remained the same: until the Revolution of 1917, the roads of Russia were dotted with pilgrims going from one shrine to another, especially the shrine of Sts Anthony and Theodosius at the Monastery of the Caves of Kiev, that of St Sergius at the Monastery of the Trinity at Zagorsk, and that of the founders of the Solovky Monastery in an island of the White Sea.[21] The most famous of these is the anonymous peasant who wandered from shrine to shrine reciting to himself the Prayer of Jesus ('Lord Jesus Christ, Son of God, have mercy on me, a sinner'), and who left us his simple reminiscences in *The Way of a Pilgrim*.[22] Russian pilgrims also went in large numbers to Jerusalem, where there were a number of Russian monasteries and hospices, and to Mount Athos; even in Bari the imperial government kept a hospice for Russians visiting the shrine of St Nicholas.

In the West after the upheavals of the Revolution pilgrimage begins to reappear. As mentioned above, many shrines were rebuilt and once again attracted pilgrims. In Latin America the shrines were usually not even disturbed, and many Republican governments proclaimed the Marian image of the region's most popular shrine as patroness of the nation. Our Lady of Guadalupe, in particular, was associated with Mexican independence; even the most anticlerical of governments has never dared close it down. But more than the traditional shrines centred on a saint's tomb or miraculous image, what has attracted pilgrims in the nineteenth and twentieth centuries has been the shrine at the site of a Marian apparition, such as La Salette, Lourdes and Fatima. These apparitions tend to have messages for the contemporary world which reinforce resistance to new and secular world views; the very incidence of frequent miracles was seen as a refutation of the nineteenth century's secular world-view of a universe governed by inflexible laws, where scientific knowledge, rather than prayer, was the key to healing.

Such apparitions were often perceived as a threat by governments based on the principles of the new era, and indeed, especially in the case of Fatima, came to be associated with opposition to 'godless' political systems.[23] In every case, however, they were to some degree countercultural; they were an affirmation of the permanent validity of a supernaturalist world-view which the triumphant secular culture wrote off as superseded and no longer credible. In this context it is significant that a number of claimed apparitions in the post-conciliar era have overtly condemned the Council's opening to the modern world, or served as a rallying point for pre-conciliar attitudes, even while their messages do not overtly reject the Council. In the pilgrims who flock to such places one often detects a thirst for certainty and for clear directions in life, as well as for emotionally convincing evidence of the supernatural.

In contrast to this is the recent revival of enthusiasm for the pilgrimage to Compostela. There the *experience* of pilgrimage is central, and the goal almost peripheral; many of the pilgrims who walked the old 'Road of the Stars' are agnostics, and among the believers many do not believe that the body in the cathedral is that of St James. Yet the pilgrimage is no mere walking tour; the experiences of liminality and solidarity produce a definite spiritual impact on the pilgrims.

In contrasting ways and for contrasting reasons, it seems that the urge to pilgrimage is still very much alive in our age. Traditional pilgrims still flock to the old tombs and icons; secular pilgrims seek the experience of liminal solidarity for its own sake; others seek reassurance that the beleaguered supernatural world-view does in fact work by seeking the places of apparitions. But all of them seem to agree instinctively that while God may be everywhere, God must sometimes be sought in special places. This instinct may best be expressed in the words of a Scottish gardener who, on meeting someone just returned from the island of Iona, sacred to the memory of the Irish missionary abbot St Columkill, remarked 'Ah, Iona is a very thin place!' When asked to explain his words, he replied, 'There's very little between Iona and the Lord.'[24] God may be in every place, but human experience across the ages (and in our own age) shows us that certain places are 'thinner', more transparent than others, so that the ubiquitous presence may be experienced there more easily and tangibly. Those who, for whatever reason, hunger to see God's face will always beat a path to such places.

Notes

1. At the crucial moment that led him on the quest for certain knowledge that culminated in the *Cogito*, Descartes vowed a pilgrimage to Loreto; an ironical beginning for modern rationalism: K. Stern, *The Flight from Woman*, London 1966, 79.

2. Augustine, *Letter* 155, PL XXXII.

3. In this context we should mention the phenomenon of the 'artificial shrine', which is simply a church that is proclaimed to be a shrine by ecclesiastical authorities or enterprising clergy, with no basis in any spontaneous and extraordinary manifestation of the sacred. These so-called shrines rarely take root in the people's hearts; there is nothing there which they could not find in their parish church.

4. See Cousins' essay 'Francis of Assisi: Christian Mysticism at the Crossroads', in S. Katz, *Mysticism and Religious Traditions*, New York and London 1983. A similar experience is described in Léon Zander, *Le Pélérinage*, Paris 1954.

5. The spot was well known, and in recent times has again become a centre of devotion for both Anglicans and Catholics.

6. N. Arseniev, *Russian Piety*, New York 1964, 142.

7. Such experiences of liminality and what we might call 'liminal solidarity' appear over and over in Ellen O. Feinberg, *Following the Milky Way*, Ames, Iowa 1989; Bettina Selby, *Pilgrim's Road*, Boston 1994; Edward F. Stanton, *Road of Stars to Santiago*, Lexington, Kentucky 1994.

8. *The Way of a Pilgrim*, trans. R. M. French, New York 1965.

9. Other examples are discussed in R. Hertz, 'St Besse: A Study of an Alpine Cult', and P. Sanchis, 'The Portuguese *Romarías*', both in S. Wilson (ed.), *Saints and Their Cults: Studies in Religious Sociology, Folklore and History*, Cambridge University Press 1983.

10. Eusebius, *Life of Constantine* III.26; Jerome, *Letter* 58.

11. Martyrdom of Polycarp, 18.2–3.

12. The legend of St Maris with his wife Martha and their sons Audifax and Avakum, noble Persians who supposedly came to Rome to venerate the graves of the apostles and were caught and executed, is late and unreliable.

13. The Dialogue against Proclus is lost, but this passage is preserved in Eusebius, *Ecclesiastical History* II.25. Gaius wrote this dialogue in the pontificate of Zephyrinus (198–217) or possibly in that of Victor I (186–197).

14. M. Guarducci, *La Tomba di Pietro*, Rome 1959. The graffiti can be dated approximately because the walls on which some of them were scratched became inaccessible as a result of later and datable construction in the area.

15. For example she, or rather her local guides, conflate Salim by the Jordan (cf. John 3.23) with Salem, the city of Melchizedek, which was actually Jerusalem; there she is shown the ruins of Melchizedek's palace and the church that marks the spot where he welcomed Abraham with the offering of bread and wine, *Peregrinatio Etheriae*, 13.4–14.3.

16. Ibid., 38.1.

17. Until the Crusades, worship in the basilicas had followed the local (Eastern) use; during the time of the Latin kingdom it followed the Western rite, but the Greeks were allowed to hold their services at certain times or in side chapels.

18. The most notorious case is the theft of the body of St Foy from Agen by the monks of Conques, which as a result became a major centre of pilgrimage.

19. It should be kept in mind, however, that medieval pilgrims could not count on the Pope's presence. Aside from the seventy years at Avignon, medieval Popes at the best of times tended to be peripatetic, spending long periods at Orvieto, Viterbo and other cities of the Papal States. Pilgrimage to the shrines of Rome was therefore distinct from going to the Curia on ecclesiastical business.

20. Gregory the Great explicitly advised Augustine of Canterbury to build churches on the sites of Anglo-Saxon shrines, and both Martin of Tours and Boniface built churches with the wood of sacred trees they had felled. The crypt of Chartres had been a shrine to the Mother Goddess since pre-Roman times. For the orthodoxy of these practised see J. Vidal, 'Towards an Understanding of Synthesis in Iberian and Hispanic American Popular Religiosity', in A. Stevens Arroyo (ed.), *An Enduring Flame: Studies in Latin Popular Religiosity*, New York 1995.

21. Arseniev, *Russian Piety* (n. 6), 15.

22. See n. 8 above. A similar case of a mystic and 'perpetual' pilgrim wandering from shrine to shrine is found in the West in St Benedict Joseph Labre.

23. This was even more clear in certain unapproved apparitions, such as Necedah in the American state of Wisconsin, whose message was primarily anti-Communist – taking Fatima to its 'logical' conclusions.

24. The story is told by the English student of mysticism Evelyn Underhill, quoted by Bishop Kallistos (Ware) of Diokleia in 'C. S. Lewis: an "Anonymous Orthodox"?', *Sobornost* 17.2, 1995, 20.

A Pilgrimage to Kailâsa and Mânasasaras

Raimon Panikkar

My pilgrimage of twenty-five days during the month of September 1994 revealed to me a threefold symbolic power of that Sacred Mountain and Holy Lake which for millennia have stood there attracting peoples and challenging religions to overcome their doctrinal 'inflations'. A pilgrimage is not theory (orthodoxy) but action (orthopraxis). I shall transfer to Kailâsa the symbolic power of a human invariant. It may be any other pilgrimage, physical, merely internal or any other ultimate experience. Kailâsa is the excuse but also the symbol.

I have politely refused to write my 'impressions' of the pilgrimage, stating that the Absolute is ineffable, and that the ineffable cannot be spoken. I went without paper, pen and camera. I went, but I did not conceptualize. What follows is just a narrative – not the 'real thing'.

1. Transcending history

Kailâsa is a temple of the Absolute. Unlike any mosque, cathedral or shrine, it is not man-made. Kailâsa simply *is*; it stands there. It has been *discovered* as a sacred symbol by most of the South Asian religions (Bon-Po, Hindus, Jainas, Buddhists, Sikhs, etc.). But it was already there.

Nobody can claim an exclusive right to Kailâsa. It is not a private property; it is not just a mass of matter covered by snow, not a geographical protuberance, far less a closed historical phenomenon. It is a sacred symbol for all those who recognize it – and by this recognition invest the mountain with a new degree of reality.

Many pilgrimages are hazardous, but this one is especially risky. You put your life at stake; you go on a path of no return. Neither modern rescue facilities are available nor the traditional ones, since the long route of pilgrimage from Katmandu, Kodari, Nyalam, etc. has practically no pilgrims. One is alone and there is no escaping from death if the heart weakens. One has to be ready to abandon history and to take leave of time.

The subjective aspect of this experience is that one has to be prepared to risk one's life – especially if one is not young and not trained in walking at high altitudes. One comes near to 6.000 metres several times. One may be theoretically ready and prepared, but when the actual experience comes, the readiness disappears and the proleptic courage is of no avail. Death is not an intellectual affair. It is simply ceasing to live – at least on this phase and in this body. Words and thoughts do not help. You simply are between being and non-being: *asti, nâsti* (*Katha Upanishad*). Death is not in you. You don't feel ill. There is no point of getting up from the sleeping bag so as to breathe better. Death is all around. It is the enveloping atmosphere which seems to embrace you from all sides with the arms of death. It is not a threat. It is an embrace which peacefully kills – although it has spared me this time.

But if during the night the subjective awareness prevails, during the day the objective awareness is overwhelming. For hours and days the scenery is timeless and the landscape is out of history. All human concerns tied to temporality dissipate. Human history, both personal and collective, sinks into irrelevance. The immense valleys, the distant peaks, the lack of trees, the rocks and rivers, the vast highlands, all exist without history. They don't come from an origin and go to an *eschaton*. They are simply present.

In our modern times, most of human existence is lived on the river-bed of history. Most of our human actions are goal-orientated and our lives are eschatologically conditioned. We seem to live for tomorrow, to work for the future and act in view of some goal to be attained in time. Death frightens because death frustrates all our projects and interrupts our dreams. We live pro-jecting, believing we go somewhere in history. All this disappears in the high plains of Tibet. It is not that history stops. History is simply not there. Life is of the present. If you have to live life to the full, you have to live it today without waiting for the morrow, without reserving energy for the future. The overwhelming presence is that of the Earth. She is there with the moon and the sun, and there are the stars that move around – smoothly and without hurry.

The pilgrim goes 'there' just to go there, just for nothing – and if one has the secret desire for 'merits' (*punya*) one is soon disappointed. The pilgrim interrupts all the chores and 'important' activities of ordinary life and is not even sure to be able to resume them after the journey.

But when the experience that this is a way of no return bounces on you,

you discover that all your historical achievements are irrelevant. Historical consciousness is one of the main factors of present-day human despair. Only a tiny minority of our competitive society has 'made it'. Only a few become director generals, top executives, world-renowned artists, workers, happily married, economically carefree, or even saints or spiritually realized persons. You have to content yourself by playing second fiddle or no fiddle at all, and may seek consolation in a future heaven, karma or the like – which only amounts to prolonging the myth of history as the canvas of reality.

When you realize that each step could be the last, you become aware that each step is definitive. It is not the last one because the next step is more difficult. You are not climbing so that the next looms more dangerous or impossible. The next step is practically like the previous one. Human life is one step after the other, and none of them is a Vishnu stride, but an ordinary one, at least up to the last conscious step. Each 'normal' 'trivial' moment could be our last. What then of our lives? Frustration, because we have not arrived? Sadness, because we have squandered the past? Or just the experience that at any moment of the way our entire life is present?

Paradoxically enough, the pilgrimage helps us realize that the way is to no-where, that it is now-here, that each step is the fulfilment of the *yâtrâ*. It is not tourism. It is the first step that counts. And each step is the first – and the last.

We sometimes tend to imagine that it is easier to feel the novelty of the first step than the ultimacy of any step. I would venture to say that there is no really *first* step if it is not equally the *last*. Otherwise, each step is just the continuation of a prior one and not really the first. We become aware that it is the first, when it dawns to our consciousness that it could be, and in a certain way is the last.

II. Sacred space

There are many sacred spots in the world, many sacred places of pilgrimage. The sacredness of Kailâsa and Mânasasaras helps us to become aware that any sacred space is unique. But their sacred character is not a confined place. It is the empty space which manifests its sacredness, i.e. its definitive reality. The wonder of the pilgrimage is that the empty space becomes visible or rather transparent: the void is filled with pure light; the space is full of emptiness. Kailâsa is not the limit, but the centre.

Yet this empty space is filled with another reality. It is filled with man. 'The *purusha* fills the All.' The pilgrim fills that space. It is a human space; that space which allows man to be free: to move outside the strait-jacket of history.

Man and nature belong together; space is their link. Man is not inside space as in a box. There is no such a box. There are plains, mountains, valleys, passes, rivers, grass, rocks, trees, animals and men . . . All belong together and space unites them all.

Man is a historical being, but not exclusively historical. Man is a cosmic being, too. Our destiny is tied to the destiny of the earth. Kailâsa is a symbol for the cosmic nature of man. Kailâsa is imposing but not threatening. Its peak is like a cupola or like a tumescent feminine breast: round, soft, snow-white, alluring, inviting, seducing. Open to the sight, but not to the touch. Beauty could be the word to sum it all up. She commands admiration, respect and awe.

Sacred space is a cosmic magnitude. Even the Christian scripture speaks of the 'new heavens and the new earth' and not only of the 'new Man'. 'Heaven and earth are held by the *Skambha*', says the *Atharva Veda*. Earth, the *devī*, is the 'Primeval Mother', sings the *Bhûmi Sûkta* of the same Veda.

The pilgrim to Kailâsa feels that cosmic oneness without pantheistic confusion. We are epiphenomena on the cosmic venture of our destiny – and deep down in our being there is the awareness of an immortality which is not the private property of our body or our soul, but the gift of the Spirit; the true *âtman* not only within us, but also at the core of any being. It is often said that we cannot enjoy divine friendship if we do not love our fellow-humans. It is often forgotten that cosmic *koinônia* is also required for our union with the divine, ultimately for being our true selves. Terrestrial estrangement brings about human alienation and divine ostracism.

III. An ultimate pilgrimage

Kalâsa is an ultimate pilgrimage, a *paramâ yâtrâ*. You don't reach Kailâsa, you don't climb the peak, you circumambulate it, you perform the *parikrama*, you do the *pradakshina*.

Like anything ultimate, this pilgrimage is ineffable. It is not beyond description because we are poor in words. It is unspeakable because its experience transcends the logos. The ultimate pilgrimage belongs to the Spirit, to the other shore of reason. It is another way of saying that it does not constrain the mind. We are in a realm which is free from logical necessity (the Greek *anagkê*), not because it is above the mind, but because it is outside it.

Ultimate means that it is a pilgrimage of no return. If you ever come back, it is sheer grace, a new being.

Since an 'ultimate' pilgrimage is indescribable, I am not going to attempt to describe it.

Instead, I shall betray what I realized *after* the experience. I had no such intentions before the pilgrimage. I have always been more inclined to the spiritual pilgrimage. Yet that memory of a Hindu father telling his teenage son about Kailâsa and Mansarovar reverberated in him when the occasion arose to join the last batch of sadhus the Chinese would allow in in 1959. He had then to renounce by virtue of 'holy' (Christian) obedience, and later on due to other reasons, not the least an incident showing that his heart could not bear high altitudes. By an inexplicable synchronicity of events he found himself this time almost led to undertake the pilgrimage which for him was likely to be not only ultimate but final . . .

A threefold transformative action underpinned my pilgrimage. I was well aware that if this metamorphosis could take place in the microcosm of my person, it would have repercussions in the macrocosm itself.

Peace between men, i.e., among religions, because there is no denying that religions have been the main causes of human strife. My pilgrimage was an ecumenical gesture; overcoming all exclusivisms (of any tradition or religion); Kailâsa is not only for Hindus. Defeating all inclusivisms (and all 'fulfilment-theologies'); Kailâsa is also for Christians, but not because of a higher right to absorb all other traditions. Resisting all solipsisms ('We do our thing and you yours – and nobody cares'); Kailâsa is for all.

In this sense, as I had done in Arunâcala and Gangotri with Swâmi Abhishiktânanda, I celebrated the cosmic sacrifice of the cross in the spirit of the Vedas, Melchisedek and all the other 'commerces' between heaven and earth, which for me was symbolized in the eucharist. Three short sentences of the Chândogya Upanishad, John's Prologue and Nâgârjuna were pronounced in the liturgy, remembering Prajâpati, Abel and Abraham, re-enacting the action of Jesus the Christ who reminded us that neither in Gerizim, nor Jerusalem, nor Kailâsa . . ., neither exclusively among Jews, Hindus, Christians, Africans . . . dwells the Spirit and the truth.

Under heaven, symbol of the divine, with a friend representing humanity, and on the earth embodying the entire creation, 'the one and single sacrifice', as the Rig Veda explicitly chants, that primordial sacred action (with bread and wine) was performed.

Peace with the earth was the second ecosophical transformation. To say that you go there to die sounds horrible and it would be wrong. To explain that you go where you also belong and do not mind accepting a *requiescat in pace* on the womb of Mother Earth is a different thing altogether. It is a transformation which I have called ecosophical: a participation in the wisdom of the earth of which man is the intelligent flowering – and speaker. It was not a journey into the abyss. It was a pilgrimage, an *itinerarium* where you also belong. *Gaia eleyson* is an indispensable human prayer in our times.

Peace among the gods was the third and still the more ambitious transformation. If the different groups of what we still call the *homo sapiens* quarrel with each other, it may well be because there is also no peace in the *devaloka*, in the pantheon of the higher spheres. The gods have not always been gods of peace. The sacrifice is not only there to appease the wrath of the gods towards us. It is also performed to establish peace in that realm as well.

I am conscious of the ambitious utopia of this religious orthopraxis. If eclecticism is the danger of the first point and anthropomorphism that of the second, substantialization of the divine would be the trap of the third. We are all engaged in a cosmotheandric adventure. How could I, little fellow, even entertain such literally sublime aspirations? I offer no excuse, because I did not choose to undertake this pilgrimage, nor had I any prior purpose of doing or thinking such things.

This issue of *Concilium* wants us to reflect on the nature and meaning of pilgrimage. Perhaps these lines may be a witnessing of what a pilgrimage can do – and the following verses may contribute to it:

> Can you not go to Kailâsa?
> Sad consolation your internal path!
> Have you gone to Mansarovar?
> Fruitless effort your way!
> Is the Way only into Self,
> because the Self is the Journey
> as Buddha and Christ saw?

Therefore:

> Don't go as if you were going;
> don't renounce as if you were renouncing.
> Be a pilgrim without pilgrimage.
> Be a pilgrim into No-where:
> Now – Here!

And yet:

Kailâsa has attracted pilgrims
for thousands of years
and from scores of religions.
'God has put you among minerals'
said to the Ka'ba a great master.
Is it only superstition?
Can a mountain not be sacred?
Should a body not be holy?
Is the Truth only a concept?
And Beauty just sentiment?
Is religion only doctrine?
And faith just ideology?
We hear it once again:
'Get up and be on your Way!'

Pilgrimage and Literature

Philippe Baud

I. Setting out

People have always loved to set out to see the world: to explore it, for their work or on holiday, for pious reasons or as a result of some secret attraction, to find food or acquire education. Setting out on a journey is a way of coping with their fears and appeasing a burning desire. The risk involved in crossing frontiers enables us to grow. All the sages repeat that 'travel trains the young'.

If they are to 'see the world', young men and women have to leave the constraints of their mothers' arms. At the same time they may feel a spiritual need, the need for a soul, which so far has been fulfilled by dreaming. This may make them seek a garden of Eden, a promised land, sometimes thought to lie in the past, sometimes thought to be ahead. Once men and women know themselves to be 'strangers and travellers on earth', they invoke geographies and ages which are often more fictitious than real. As they set out, they challenge both the constraints of the 'establishment' and the security offered by frontiers. Beyond the horizons imposed on them, they go in quest of their grail, seek their native country, certain that 'true life is elsewhere'. The human condition is certainly that of a pilgrim. So it is not surprising that the societies which seek to affirm the sacral character of their power forbid access to places of pilgrimage, make the nomads settle down, imprison the curious, gag writers, curse poets, and burn visionaries, offering only exile as a possible route. The strong-minded, the scapegoats, have to die outside the world so that their brothers and sisters can sleep soundly.

Whether an explorer or a fugitive (very rarely a dilettante before the modern tourist industry), the traveller thus becomes an initiate. To deserve this title – the 'shell' of the pilgrims of St James – day by day the traveller has to risk 'beginning after beginning': to ride out storms, confront dangers, overcome various obstacles, cross 'devil's bridges', and kill fiery dragons. This has given rise to travellers' tales, which of course have epic dimensions – the voyages of heroes and gods which are undertaken so willingly in all mythologies. In fact these travels are a 'religious' activity: they link the inhabitants of heaven with those of earth, just as they bring men closer together. Can peoples know one another if they scorn one another's gods? For all that, every Odyssey or peregrination is surrounded by rituals: the auguries are consulted, sacrifices are made on departure, prayers are offered against the evil spirits of the way, there are gestures on arrival. For here we have a journey to meet the 'other', indeed an approach to the 'Wholly Other', in a country of formidable powers, usually described as 'the Beyond'. As a result, popular piety feels the need to venerate the 'itinerant' saints, with Christopher, patron of travellers, at their head. By opening their doors to those who are on the road, Christians welcome an envoy of God, Christ himself. The trials relating to the 'knowledge of good and evil' which mark the way offer an effective initiation. Pilgrimages are undertaken like that of Tannhäuser, seized with vertigo every time he found himself at the junction of the roads to Rome or the Venusberg, fall and purification, lapse and conversion. On the way to the source, life is renewed and at last reveals its meaning.

The intoxication of the first discoveries is followed by weariness and disenchantment. Odysseus, after so many adventures, returns to the family home to spend the rest of his life with his kinsfolk. Fortified by experiences, from then on the heroes can dream of becoming 'sages'. Memories are transformed, take on bright colours, provoke images. The imaginary wins out over the real: this is the way in which epics, tales, romances and poems come into being. The legend comes to tell 'the truth', the fable is the basis for history; the pages of a 'personal diary' are regarded as sacred relics: the whole of life can become an Odyssey. This leads to the desire to be descended from a mythical hero, a 'wandering Aramaean', who provides us with a model and is like a child of our own.

II. The call

As they set out, pilgrims are responding to a call which summons them from within rather than from outside. Though on their way to an encounter, in their hearts they are already there: each stage anticipates the meeting. Far from seeking to 'get away from it all', they dimly know that their pilgrimage is in a way 'back to the beginning' – next year in

Jerusalem! – and that the whole of life is a pilgrimage. A basic nostalgia guides their steps towards a 'holy land' from which all suffering will be banished: the garden of the Hesperides or Montsalvat. On this way privations can prove riches, weariness can lead to new strength, once the pilgrim accepts the possibility of never returning, or at least of not returning *the same*.

A similar call prompted the children of the mad crusade of 1212, just as today young people, disillusioned with the post-industrial West, escape to the slopes of Katmandu in quest of their vanished gods. In 1298, when he published his *Book*, Marco Polo inspired people to go on voyages of discovery and mission, or rather voyages of 'conquest'. In the industrial age, fascinated by the messianic perspectives opened up by technical progress, Jules Verne took his readers 'to the centre of the earth', 'to the moon' and 'twenty thousand leagues under the sea'.[1] A good fifty years later, Céline invited readers on a *Journey to the End of Night* (1932), a bitter epic of pitiful and burlesque figures who are so desperately human. *The Human Comedy*[2] has become a tragedy in a world devoted to hatred and war. After the one-way trains to Auschwitz and the Hiroshima bomb, a new generation of pilgrims is arising, responding to the sound and fury of life by organizing peace marches, while the mass of citizens continue to go off on their seasonal migrations to beaches or snow-covered slopes.

The journey to the realm of the dead doubtless inspired the living to tell their first travel stories. The wanderings of the tribal chiefs could not stop abruptly when they returned to the land of their ancestors: they had to keep on travelling, fighting, confronting the fears and trials of those who had the audacity to survive them. The living had to be able to recognize their own footprints in the throng of their heroes or their gods. The bard – Orpheus – became the one who passed between these worlds, linked together, but with no communication between them. The one who sang and spoke opened up the way, but though he penetrated the 'other world', he could not stop or look back.

III. The first Christian pilgrims

Pilgrimage leads to stories which sooner or later are written down; reading such stories leads to discussion which in turn prompts new pilgrims to set off. There is a specific pilgrimage literature: sometimes, in the form of guides for pilgrims, it offers maps and practical advice, like today's tourist guides; sometimes, in the form of memoirs, it bears witness, offers a collection of the best memories. When Helena, the mother of the emperor Constantine, went to Palestine in September 326, she unwittingly inaugurated a type of journey which was to develop in an extraordinary fashion: 'pilgrimages to the Holy Land', which were also an extension of the Jewish tradition of 'ascents to Jerusalem'. Barely seven years later, an anonymous author known as the 'Pilgrim of Bordeaux' produced the first journal of such a journey.[3] This *Itinerarium a Burdigala Jerusalem usque* is an outline of the route which took him from Aquitaine to Palestine. All the distances are meticulously counted, in French leagues and Roman miles, with a variety of useful pieces of information, as if the traveller had covered so many miles in two years with the sole aim of checking that the holy places conformed to the image that he had gained of them from reading the Bible. Nothing which he was shown surprised him: neither the 'trees planted by the patriarch Jacob' near the well of Shechem, nor the 'palm trees from which the children cut branches to throw them in the steps of Jesus on his entry into Jerusalem'. However, in 325 St Jerome had already written from Bethlehem to St Paulinus of Nola, also from Bordeaux: 'Don't imagine that your faith lacks anything because you have not seen Jerusalem.'[4] Having left the cultivated salons of Rome for the solitude of Palestine, Jerome never took any other pilgrimage to the 'Holy Land' than that which led to the Christ who lived within him.

It is worth mentioning here the valuable *Travel Journal* which was written towards the end of this fourth century by a devout woman named Etheria. She travelled from Galicia to Jerusalem, crossing Egypt and the Sinai desert. Her journal is an invaluable source of information about the sanctuaries which she visited, and more particularly about the liturgical life, the calendar and the rites of the Holy City. Anyone interested in the history of the churches must not fail to study the pilgrimage chronicles.

See Jerusalem! From the fourth century, this was the desire of innumerable Christians, once safer ways were opened to them. However, like present-day tourists in a hurry, pilgrims of former times were given more the stereotyped anecdotes of a guide than accurate information. In order not to disappoint their expectations, at all costs they had to be shown the sites: not only those mentioned in the Gospels, but those that popular piety wanted to see and touch: the inn at Cana; Lazarus's, not to mention Veronica's, house; and the school that Mary once went to. Stories came to be attached to all these places to which pilgrims flocked in order to venerate a tomb or touch a relic; and once these things had been set down in writing they became *legenda*, i.e. 'what can be read'. That is how the legends appeared, stories about holy figures which were destined to be read during matins on their respective feast days.

This literature developed especially in places of pilgrimage, to prompt or preserve testimonies to healings or miracle stories, giving examples of life and faith to believers which had been richly embellished. Around 1265, a Dominican from Geneva, Jacques de Voragine, collected these fables under the title *Legenda Sanctorum*. The work, which in the fifteenth century was to become the *Golden Legend*, was a great success and inspired many paintings: it was one of the first to benefit from the invention of printing. Out of a desire to edify, the miraculous elements in it won out over realism, leading to excesses and a fervour which were soon to be found in the *chansons de geste* and the romances of chivalry, right down to the time when Cervantes depicted his ultimate figure of legend, a ridiculous saint in armour, Don Quixote, who was more besotted with chivalry than his contemporaries were besotted with Christ.

IV. The Middle Ages

In 634, taking advantage of the collapse of the Byzantine empire and fortified by their recent conversion to Islam, the Arabs invaded Palestine and Syria. Under the government of the Umayyad caliphs of Damascus and then the Abbasids of Baghdad, the Holy Land enjoyed four centuries of relative peace. The land was then conquered in the tenth century by the Fatimids of Egypt, and in 1076 Jerusalem was captured by the formidable Seldjuks, who came from Turkey. It became too risky for Western Christians to set out for Jerusalem. So it is not surprising that we now see new pilgrimage routes being developed, prompted by the discovery of the bodies of saints. The miraculous discovery of the tomb of a figure who had long been venerated could draw pilgrims to the ends of the earth. At that time on Cape Finistère (*finis terrae*), the tomb of the apostle James was discovered! Hagiographical legends flourished to make up for the lack of authenticity. There is no need to emphasize here the enormous importance of the pilgrimage to Compostela throughout the Middle Ages; this importance was not only cultural and social but also spiritual and ecclesial. From the ninth century onwards, right across Europe but more specifically between France and Spain, the routes of St James became main thoroughfares for the exchange of ideas and knowledge: religious architecture, painting and music largely benefited from this. These pilgrimages equally prompted literary work leading to the production of pilgrimage guides and other books. To see how important they were and how much interest there was in them we need only look at the rich variety of themes discussed in the books that form the *Liber Sancti Jacobi*:[5] I. an anthology of liturgical pieces, a collection of sermons, offices and hymns in honour of the apostles; II. a Book of Miracles; III. The Book of the Translation, a long account of the evangelization of Spain by St James, followed by the martyrdom of the apostle and his legend; IV. The History of Charlemagne and Roland; and V. a pilgrim's guide to St James of Compostella, a compendium of practical advice for pilgrims, indicating where to stop, what relics to venerate and what sanctuaries to visit before reaching the cathedral of Compostella. In addition to its hagiographical interest, the last volume alone offers valuable information about topography, human geography, history and philology.

The First Crusade (1096–1099), preached by Urban II, reopened the routes to the Holy Land. Foolish but initially disinterested enterprises, these armed pilgrimages quickly degenerated into expeditions of conquest. By developing a penchant for heroic stories, these warlike adventures also inspired a vast literature which exalted faith and bravery in fights against 'the infidels'. In their *chansons de geste* (from the Latin *gesta*, actions), the troubadours celebrated the military exploits of Carolingian heroes as if they were the prowess of Crusader knights. This led to the composition of new epics like the *Chanson de Roland*, in which the ride of Charlemagne's rearguard became a crusade and their ambushing by a troop of Basque mountainfolk the gigantic attack of 400,000 Saracen cavalry.

Around 1910, Joseph Bédier, the great French medievalist, revived literary theories about the formation of French epics by noting the close links between the various places mentioned in the *chansons de geste* and the stopping places on the great pilgrimages. His famous thesis is well summed up by the adage 'in the beginning was the route'. In the abbeys and the sanctuaries where the pilgrims rested, admiring sarcophagi, inscriptions and tombs, monks and clerks were charged with 'making the stones speak', in order to satisfy the curiosity of these pilgrims and to entertain them. In this way, it is said, epic material was formed and grew; it was soon carried by the wandering entertainers along the pilgrimage routes, until a more talented poet or narrator gave the amplified epic a definitive written form. When the places and the objects did not give rise to a story, if need be a new 'relic' could be invented to substantiate the text: on the route to Spain the pilgrim could thus admire the tomb of Roland at Blaye and his elephant at Saint-Seurin de Bordeaux.

Seductive though this thesis was, it was nevertheless contested:

according to other experts the poems did not originate in local legends; on the contrary, the legends were prompted by literary works. However, regardless of the purely literary problem of the origins of the *chanson de geste*, no one can deny the important role played by pilgrimages in the development and diffusion of medieval literature.

The influence exercised on it by the Crusades was quite as decisive. Just as the Crusades brought spices into the kitchen, so they introduced two new tastes into French literature, which were full of promise for the future: the historical chronicle and exoticism. People in the West were eager to hear authentic stories of these great Eastern adventures, composed by those who had witnessed them with their own eyes. So the 'old soldiers' were encouraged to write their memoirs. Ceasing to be a scholarly work or a romantic evocation of events, history was to find its definitive language here: French prose, fluent and precise. As they sat down to read the great chroniclers of expeditions to the Holy Land – Geoffroi de Villehardouin (1150–1213), Robert de Clary (1170–1216) and Jean de Joinville (1224–1317), a confidant of St Louis, readers from a Western Christendom which believed itself to be the centre of the world discovered the existence of other horizons, other civilizations and other believers.

V. The Arab world

During the same period, Arabic literature also saw the development of a particular literary genre which arose out of stories of pilgrims to Mecca: the *rihla*, 'journal' or travel 'account', providing itineraries and descriptions of pilgrimage routes. Because of the host of political, social and economic observations which can be gleaned from the route, these accounts are very valuable geographical and historical documents. Though their authors are particularly concerned to describe the Holy Places – Mecca and Medina – they also seek to share the feeling of disorientation among those who visit the great centres of Islam. Ibn Jubayr (1145–1217) became the unparalleled master of the genre, combining his picturesque vision of the world through which he travelled with a wealth of religious documentation. One might also mention the name of Ibn Battuta (1304–1377), a great writer for whom pilgrimage was certainly no more than a pretext for setting out to discover the world. Walking the roads of Spain, North Africa, Asia Minor, India, Russia and China for twenty-five years, this indefatigable traveller saw so many strange things and met so many famous persons that he found it difficult to stem the flow of his memories. The years pass and the difficulties of the road are forgotten as he dictates to his secretary the *rihla* of his travels, reliving his long journey and recreating the real through the imaginary.

VI. Pilgrimage in India

But in what country of the world do the roads see the passage of more pilgrims than India? Today along the tarmac, as formerly along the sandy tracks, pilgrims go by routes which seem to have been created solely to link the temples. In groups or alone, they sing, since by singing they remain alone with God, even in the midst of the crowd.

India has been educated by its great pilgrims. Every holy place includes numerous monasteries where the original spiritual teachings are developed and handed down, and the incessant and innumerable visitors spread them all over the continent. That explains the profound cohesion of a Hinduism practised by 300 million Indians, despite the luxuriance of the local variations. To hand down their teachings, the 'spiritual masters' (only those who have gone on pilgrimage can aspire to the dignity of guru) invented a particular poetic form, the 'seamless song', or *abhanga*, which aims to harmonize the thought of the pilgrim with the slow rhythm of his step. So as not to tire the memory, the poem can be extended indefinitely, depending on the inspiration of the singer, by virtue of its refrain: one theme and one image guarantee its unity. Tukaram (1598–1650) was the master of this form. His mystical songs, handed down from generation to generation by disciples who were specifically called 'pilgrims', form a book of psalms which recalls the prayers sung by the Jewish crowds as they ascended to Jerusalem:

'Lord, let me be a small stone, a large stone or dust on the way to Panharpur, to be trodden on by the feet of the saints.'[6]

VII. Spiritual pilgrimage

Thus the figure of the pilgrim has become the symbol of the spiritual quest in a great variety of religious traditions. There is a wealth of literary examples. For Angelus Silesius (1624–1677), faithful to the current of a negative theology, and heir of Eckhart and Tauler in a baroque Germany, the inner man – the cherubic pilgrim – is a wanderer who has to seek God always beyond what his spirit can grasp of God. In *The Way of a Pilgrim* (composed between 1856 and 1861), Orthodox spirituality has a marvellous introductory treatise on the 'Jesus prayer', offering an introduction to Hesychasm which is practicable and easily accessible. It is as a *Pilgrimage to the Sources* (1943) that Lanza del Vasto presents his itinerary of a spiritual discovery achieved through the slaveries of the modern world and violence. Paulo Coelho's *The Alchemist* (1988), which quite conventionally took up the scheme of the 'inner pilgrimage' in an edifying tale in the style of the new age, became a bestseller, and recently, with *The Wonderful Adventures of Nils*, Selma Lagerlöf has presented the theme of the initiatory journey in a Scandinavian fable: the capricious child becomes a man by sharing in the migration of the wild geese.

But of all the pilgrimages in literature, imaginary or theological, the most universal, the most finished, example is certainly that which Dante (1265–1321) followed in his *Comedy*, to which posterity attached the epithet 'Divine'. The odyssey is that of the poet, lost 'in the middle of the way of life' in the dark forest of sin, and rescued from peril by the intercession of Beatrice. His saving pilgrimage into the other world is guided first by Virgil (*Hell* and *Purgatory*) and then by Beatrice herself (*Paradise*). The course of the poem with its 14,229 lines follows the pattern of his personal destiny, which is made a model for the Christian vocation. Integrating into his destiny the way previously covered by the whole 'human family', Dante deciphers the history of the world as that of a freedom which is gradually discovered in the immovable divine will. The goal of the pilgrimage, begun in the raptures of the feelings of a lover, can only be in God, in this 'love which guides the sun and all the stars'.

When the 'great Romantics' evoke their 'Years of Pilgrimage',[7] they express more their 'discontent with life' than a thirst for encounter or discovery. Their spiritual quest remains diffuse and quite subjective. Their holy places are caves or waterfalls, ancient or medieval ruins, craggy peaks or moonlit streams. This natural sense of religion – a pietism on the periphery of any revelation which is not intimate or personal – leads them to seek a paradisal age, the celebration of a primordial time, a privileged or fundamental era, which detaches itself as a 'golden age' from the busy fresco of history. They set sail for immortal Greece or the sun of Italy, go up to the sources of the Nile, or venture among the 'good savages' of America or elsewhere. Their voyages are made as much in dreams as in reality; new horizons elevate the imagination and provide promising themes for writing. The wise Goethe crosses the Alps to escape – very briefly – his followers, his duties, his reputation, finally to discover at the age of thirty-seven the simple joy of living; and Byron, Shelley, Nerval and many others, enamoured of freedom, driven by ambition or dogged by a heavy anxiety, set out to exorcise their fear of 'exile'. Fleeing towards more space and sun, these restless figures try to understand themselves better, to discover themselves – and this is attested by numerous travel notebooks, private diaries, dramatic compositions, elegies and poems – which at the same time bear witness to the original wandering.

Chateaubriand's stay in the Holy Land (from 4 to 12 October 1806 – he devoted just one day to a visit to Jerusalem) was more in haste, much less premeditated than he gives us to suppose. His curiosity about 'Moorish antiquities' was in fact an urge to join a lady who was waiting for him in Granada. 'But since I have got this far,' he writes from Constantinople, 'I have to go to Jerusalem.' This detour to Palestine proved useful for the author of the *Genius of Christianity*. As for his descriptions of the countryside, he was content to pillage the works of travellers before him without acknowledgment.

VII. Conclusion

Aren't writers and lovers of books pilgrims from their birth? As their eyes follow the ink marks, the spirits are free to escape to 'another world', 'another time', a country of their childhood or their imagination. Though linked with other invisible readers and thus having a strange sense of belonging, they travel alone with their 'books' through the human community, choosing their routes, stopping where they think appropriate, and are confronted with themselves in their quest for meaning. Through writing or reading they experience emotions, receive lessons, share destinies, cross frontiers, hear universal questions. This is a demanding enterprise which requires solitude, perseverance and silence. Paradoxically, it is by detaching themselves from the world through which they are passing that pilgrims prepare themselves for the 'encounter'.

Translated by John Bowden

Notes

1. Jules Verne, *Journey to the Centre of the Earth* (1864); *From the Earth to the Moon* (1865); *Twenty Thousand Leagues under the Sea* (1869); *Around the Moon* (1871); *The Mysterious Island* (1895).

2. The title given by Honoré de Balzac in 1841 to his series of novels.

3. *Itinera Hierosolymitana*, CSEL XXXIX, Vienna 1898, 3–33.

4. Letters 58.2.

5. This work, composed around 1139, was published in its entirety for the first time only in 1882.

6. Tukartam, *Psalms of the Pilgrim*, 89.

7. The title of a cycle for piano (definitive edition 1855) which Franz Liszt's journeys in Switzerland and Italy inspired him to compose.

II · The Spirituality of Pilgrimage

The Immigrant Poor: On Pilgrimage to a More Human Existence

José Oscar Beozzo

I. Nomads of the new millennium

Human mobility has become the trade mark of our age. In 1995, the airlines alone transported around 1.2 billion people, more than a fifth of the world population. Cars, buses, trains and ships carried even greater numbers from one country to another, or from one part of a country to another. A good half of the world population was thus involved in spatial displacement, on longer or shorter journeys in the form of tourism, now the largest industry and source of revenue in many countries, this intensive population movement is encouraged and subsidized. France alone takes in more than 60 million foreign tourists every year, while Switzerland welcomes a tourist influx of more than twice its native population.

Fugitives

On top of this, there are other less pleasant and enjoyable displacements, unwanted by the people who undergo them, the fruits of wars, ethnic cleansing, natural and economic disasters, all swelling the tide of refugees and fugitives. The number of refugees has doubled in the last ten years, reaching 18.2 million, of which a third are in Africa, where the tragedies of Burundi, Ruanda, Liberia and Somalia have made the headlines, while those of Mozambique and Angola, engulfed in wars of independence followed by civil war for more than three decades, have faded from the news. In Asia, refugees from Afghanistan abound; in the Middle East, Palestinians, Kurds and those displaced by the Gulf War; in Europe, refugees from the war in ex-Yugoslavia and the conflicts in the former

Soviet Union (Armenia with Azerbaijan, Russia with Chechenya); in Latin America, those of the wars in Central America, especially Guatemala, where a peace agreement has still not been reached. Besides these refugees, a further 25 million people have been internally displaced in countries at war.[1]

Economic and illegal immigrants

Furthermore, there are poor immigrants, struggling to survive, desperately seeking a place in the sun, in countries with more flourishing economies, swelling the mass of unqualified workers who feed the labour black market. These are the legions of 'undocumented' Mexicans, Haitians, Dominicans and other Latin Americans and Caribbeans in the United States; in Western Europe, they make up the mass of so-called 'economic refugees' or 'illegal immigrants' coming from Eastern Europe and Africa. In an increasingly hostile climate of public opinion, foreigners are ever more discriminated against, imprisoned or expatriated in the most summary procedures, with no right of appeal. The Decree 187 passed in California in 1994 excluded some 1.7 million undocumented workers, together with their wives and children, from the public education and welfare systems. At the recent UN Conference on Population and Development, held in Cairo in 1994, the press concentrated on the issues of abortion, access to contraception and the affirmation of reproductive rights, but produced very little coverage of the lively debates on the subjects of development and the right to immigration and protection of immigrants and refugees, vital to the less developed countries and to people involved in such situations. Even on the subject of legal immigrants, such a crucial topic for families, it was not possible to extract from the wealthy nations more than a statement that 'family reunification forms an important factor in international immigration'. The broad recommendation was added that persons belonging to the same family should have the right to be reunited, without this being accepted as an obligation on states.[2]

The same world that encourages free movement of capital, merchandise and tourists closes brutally against poor refugees and immigrants, with increasingly restrictive legislation, even when not tainted with xenophobia and thinly disguised racism. The institution of 'humanitarian refuge', with its roots in the biblical 'cities set apart' (cf Deut. 19.1–13), is currently in crisis, replaced by laws that drastically restrict its application and are, in practice, becoming laws not for sheltering but for summary deportation of refugees.

We can summarize the present-day scene by saying that, in poor countries, there is growing pressure to emigrate, as a means of escaping the civil wars, ethnic and religious cleansings, tortures, violence and political assassinations, unemployment and lack of means of economic survival. At the same time, in the richer countries, there are increased barriers against taking in refugees, and legal restrictions on poor immigrants are being multiplied.

Exodus from the countryside to the cities

Besides this international migration, the countries of the South are experiencing a more dramatic form of the great European phenomenon of the nineteenth century and early decades of the twentieth: internal migration from the countryside to the cities. The landless are abandoning rural areas and coming to fill urban zones, living in ever more precarious conditions. Cities such as Sao Paulo have gone from a tiny urban centre with fewer than 20,000 inhabitants a little over a hundred years ago to a megalopolis bordering on 20 million today. There, millions live in swarming slums, under bridges and viaducts, in streets with no roof over their heads, in the worst cases – and these are legion. Calcutta, Delhi and Bombay in India; Djakarta in Indonesia; Cairo, Lagos, Kinshasa and Johannesburg in Africa; Mexico City, Caracas, Bogotá, Lima, Santiago, Buenos Aires, Rio de Janeiro and Sao Paulo in Latin America: all show the same pattern of overcrowding – precarious dwellings and urban squalor, aggravated by unemployment and the collapse of public services brought about by the new wave of neo-liberal economic policies. In Brazil today, around a third of the population live away from their places of origin.

Seasonal migrants

There are still those subject to seasonal migrations, seeking work and moving to the great harvests of grapes, oranges, maize, sugar cane, coffee, tobacco and other products that require abundant work forces at times, or settling in precarious encampments around huge public works: dams and barrages, hydro-electrics and railways. Then there are those who are permanently in transit: sailors, airline pilots, long-distance truckers, multi-national executives, plus those who have made nomadism their traditional way of life, such as the gypsies.

Pilgrims and religious wanderers

Finally, there are those who displace themselves for religious reasons, gathering on the banks of the Ganges in Hinduism, journeying to Mecca in Islam, or to the great pilgrimage centres in Christianity – Rome, Assisi, Lourdes, Compostela, Fatima, Guadalupe in Mexico, Aparecida in Brazil, the Holy Land and, above all, Jerusalem, meeting-point of and stand-off point between the three great monotheistic religions of Judaism, Islam and Christianity. Major causes today unite believers and unbelievers in new pilgrim movements: marches for peace in Assisi and Sarajevo; blacks marching on Washington against racial discrimination; land pilgrimages in Brazil, promoted by the 'landless' claiming a piece of soil to plant in order to live; the 'cry of the excluded', a march promoted by the social pastors of Brazil to denounce the exclusion that has been forced on the poor through neo-liberal policies of structural adjustment.

In a very particular way, we must here include messianic migrations of those indigenous peoples such as the Guaraní, who, from the sixteenth century down to today, have been continually setting out in search of the 'land without evils'. This exodus is produced by the prophecies of their shamans, who, persuaded that the end of the world is at hand, exhort their compatriots to seek refuge in the 'land-where-you-do-not-die', where the young will keep their youth and the land yield up its fruits without hard labour.

II. The spirituality of poor immigrants

A land flowing with milk and honey

In its origins, the spirituality of poor immigrants carries much of the experience of Abraham and the promises of the Exodus: taking risks, setting out from one's own land in search of a better land for oneself and one's family: 'I have come down to deliver them from the Egyptians and to bring them up out of that land to a good and broad land, a land flowing with milk and honey . . .' (Exod. 3.8).

The departure is inspired, in the first instance, by the quest for survival. In this departure, there is nothing romantic and the poor are left very little choice. Immigrants leave their own land only under pressure of the harshest necessity. Such are the sons of Jacob who leave for Egypt in search of bread, running the risk of not being accepted, of being ill-treated and deceived (Gen. 42–45); such are those 'deported' to Babylon (II Chron. 36) and, in modern times, those who migrate illegally, take up clandestine and often semi-slave work, prostitution and other degrading forms of exploitation, simply clinging to hope of survival.

Homeless and landless but rooted in hope

The dreams that encouraged immigrants before they set out quickly turn into the nightmare of discrimination, so well expressed by Ecclesiasticus: 'It is a miserable life to go from house to house; as a guest you should not open your mouth; you will play the host and provide drink without being thanked, and besides this you will hear rude words . . . ' (29.24–25).

The lot of immigrants in a foreign land is a harsh one and forms the basic subject of the First Letter of Peter to the 'exiles' or *paroikoi*,[3] the Christians dispersed and lost in the cities and towns of Asia Minor, in the inhospitable uplands of present-day Turkey. The letter seeks to encourage and sustain them in the face of contempt and discrimination, being reviled (4.14), suffering unjustly (2.19), being maligned (3.19) on account of being foreigners and Christians. The author recommends: 'Do not fear what they fear, and do not be intimidated' (3.14); 'Conduct yourselves honourably among the Gentiles, so that, though they malign you as evildoers, they may see your honourable deeds and glorify God when he comes to judge' (2.12).

Peter, faced with the defencelessness of these Christians 'with no roof and no land', insists that they build a community as the 'home' of the 'homeless', and that they show welcome and hospitality to one another: 'Be hospitable to one another without complaining' (4.9).

The contrast between dream and reality, the experience of numerous failures and the difficulty of integrating and prospering, all threaten poor immigrants with discouragement and despair. If their precarious state makes them appreciate and value solidarity, the basis of their spiritual experience lies in the question: how to keep hope alive in difficult and adverse times?

So the virtue that affects immigrants is ultimately hope, the virtue that keeps them moving forward. This is what prevents them from falling into despair, from lying down on the ground, makes them get up and set out on the road, like Elijah on the way to Horeb (1 Kings 19).

'Restore our fortunes, O Lord, like the watercourses in the Negeb' (Ps. 126.4)

Finally, it is the dream of returning that nourishes and sustains immigrants: not just the dream of setting out in search of a more human and a happier life, but also the dream of returning to one's native land. This is what keeps hope alive from day to day. Immigrants rarely set out with no thought of ever returning. They set out in the hope of coming back to their country, their family, their people, repeating the experience of the Israelite exiles:

> When the Lord restored the fortunes of Zion,
>   we were like those who dream.
> Then our mouth was filled with laughter
>   and our tongue with shouts of joy (Ps. 126.1–2).

Aliens and exiles

The ultimate characteristic of the spirituality of immigrants stems from the deep experience of being 'aliens and exiles '(I Peter 2.11), of the fact that here we have no permanent dwelling place and that there is a better and final land waiting for us, in a radical openness to the transcendent, as the Letter to the Hebrews states: 'All these died in faith without having received the promises, but from a distance they saw and greeted them. They confessed that they were strangers and foreigners on the earth . . . ' (Heb. 11.13). It also encourages us with the example of Moses, who 'persevered, as though he saw him who is invisible' (11.27).

It is the 'foreign' condition of all human existence that made St Augustine exclaim: *'inquietum est cor nostrum donec requiescat in te'*, 'our hearts are restless until they rest in you', and made St Thomas place the category of *homo viator*, 'pilgrim man', at the heart of his *Summa Theologica*. This led Thomas to a fine perception of the backdrop against which the theological virtues operate. While faith is the starting point and beginning of all Christian experience; while charity is, in itself, the greatest virtue (see I Cor. 13.13), hope is nevertheless the first virtue of *homo viator* in his earthly pilgrimage.

Charles Péguy, in his 'Porche de la troisième vertu' ('Gateway to the third virtue'), comes to a similar perception:

> *'La foi que j'aime le mieux', dit Dieu, 'c'est l'espérance.*
> *la petite espérance s'avance entre ses deux grandes soeurs et on ne*
>   *prend seulement pas garde à elle.*
> *Sur le chemin du salut, sur le chemin charnel, sur le chemin rabouteux*
>   *du salut, sur la route interminable,*
> *sur la route entre ses deux soeurs la petite espérance*
>   *s'avance,*
> *Et au milieu entre ses deux grandes soeurs, elle a l'air de se laisser*
>   *traîner.*
> *Comme un enfant qui n'aurait pas la force de marcher.*

Et que l'on traînerait sur cette route malgré elle.
Et en réalité c'est elle qui fait marcher les deux autres.
Et qui les traîne.
Et qui fait marcher tout le monde
  et qui les traîne' (22 Oct. 1911).

['The faith I like best,' says God, 'is hope. Little hope coming forward between her two big sisters, the only one we don't notice. On the road of salvation, on the fleshly road, on the rough road of salvation, on the endless road, on the road between her two big sisters, little hope moves forward . . . And between her two big sisters, she looks as if she is being pulled along, like a child who can't walk any more, being pulled along the road despite herself. And in fact it is she who is making the two others walk, and who is pulling them along, and who is making everyone walk, and pulling them along.']

III. The challenge of welcome, of hospitality and solidarity

'And when was it that we saw you as a stranger and welcomed you?'
(Matt. 25.39)

The presence of immigrants challenges our indifference to the suffering and anguish of those who are strangers, temporary among us, foreign to the culture, race or religion of the country to which they have come. Poor immigrants force us to question ourselves about the causes that determine massive exoduses of peoples and social groupings.

The challenge of immigration is not just economic or political. It is also spiritual. It is a matter of creating a counterpart to the spirituality of poor immigrants, of building a spiritual reciprocity on the part of those who live in regions, countries and cities to which immigrants come.

At the present time, there is a growing reaction of hostility, discrimination, rejection and even persecution and physical violence against foreign immigrants, with the risk of bringing back, in Europe, the old 'pogroms' against Jews, now directed against foreigners in general and Muslims in particular: Algerians, Moroccans, Tunisians, Turks, Bosnians. In the United States, the targets of discrimination are still the blacks and, now, Latin Americans and Asiatics; in Asia and Australia, the Chinese and Vietnamese; in Brazil, Bolivians, plus internal immigrants from the north-east in the south of the country. 'Ethnic cleansings' in the former Yugoslavia and the tribal massacres in black Africa are hardly good omens for the future.

The creation and cultivation of a spirituality of welcome and hospitality, of compassion and solidarity, is an urgent and necessary task. This spirituality would have to be more deeply rooted in a quest for greater justice in international relations and more equality and solidarity among nations.

There are objective difficulties in the economic sphere, as well as political and cultural ones, in the way of welcoming immigrants. The current world crisis of unemployment makes it difficult to absorb new workers, especially those lacking any professional qualifications. Differences of language, religion and culture create powerful barriers to understanding between people; preconceptions and ancestral hatreds are stirred up by right-wing parties, by the press and television, anxious to find reasons and scapegoats for the increase in urban violence, in insecurity, in unemployment or for economic recession. Precisely within this atmosphere unfavourable to welcome, what is at stake for Christians is, in the first place, their own conception of God. How can we reject strangers and continue praying to God who 'executes justice for the orphan and the widow, and who loves the strangers, providing them food and clothing' (Deut. 10.18), who promises 'glory, honour and peace for everyone who does good, the Jew first and also the Greek. For God shows no partiality' (Rom. 2.10–11). How can we face the first judge who will call us to account: 'I was a stranger and you did not welcome me' (Matt. 25.43), or who commands us to follow the example of the Samaritan (Luke 10.25–37), who goes out of his way to succour and save a foreigner?

'Remember that you were a slave in the land of Egypt' (Deut. 24.18,22)

For lack of a better argument, God resorts to history, to open a breach in the ethnocentrism of ancient Israel, an ethnocentrism which we go on reproducing in our cultures and churches. In present-day Europe a clear distinction has been drawn, with the legislation and repressive measures that stem from it, between political and economic refugees. States are willing – though reluctantly – to recognize the right of the former to shelter and protection, owing to the risks of losing their life, being imprisoned or ill-treated, which they would run in their country of origin. Economic refugees, however, are denied any rights, even though their lives may be equally at risk through lack of the means of subsistence in their country or region, which may be affected by drought, war or economic recession. Legislators and public easily forget that some 70 million Europeans migrated between 1870 and 1914, to North America,

Brazil, Uruguay, Argentina, South Africa and Australia, impelled by hunger or unemployment, the mirror image of economic refugees today. It is worth remembering the warning in Deuteronomy: 'You shall not deprive a resident alien or an orphan of justice . . . Remember that you were a slave in Egypt and the Lord God redeemed you from there; therefore I command you to do this' (24.17–18); and again: 'You shall also love the stranger, for you were strangers in the land of Egypt' (10.19).

This memory is not totally extinguished: I was deeply moved, arriving in the German city of Neuwied, late at night, to find young people holding a vigil in the cold, in front of a hostel for foreign immigrants, to guarantee their safety and peace in the face of a wave of neo-Nazi assaults which had resulted in similar residences in other German cities being set on fire. In the same spirit, in Italy civil disobedience by some communities and by Caritas itself has guaranteed shelter and protection to Albanian and African immigrants, threatened with expulsion by the government. In the United States, during the 1980s, the Sanctuary Movement helped thousands of Salvadorean refugees escaping from the military régime in their country, which was financed, trained and armed by the US government, by taking them in, hiding them and helping them to get across the frontier into Canada.

Such gestures and spaces of welcome resurrect the virtue of hospitality, so central to nomadic life, which needs to be rediscovered, in its fullness, as a mystery of God who appears and visits us in the person of the foreigner. The Letter to the Hebrews recalls this in a striking image: 'Do not neglect to show hospitality to strangers, for by doing that some have entertained angels without knowing it' (13.2). For God to become visible in a strange land, there has to be welcome, sharing and solidarity.

Translated by Paul Burns

Notes

1. For more complete data on international immigration and refugees, see the articles 'Population and Population Movements: International Migration; Refugees', in *Encyclopedia Britannica, Book of the Year*, 1994, 1995.

2. 'Governments are urged to promote, through family reunion, the normalization of the family life of legal migrants who have the right to long-term residence', in 'United Nations International Conference on Population and Development: Programme of Action' (unofficial information version), 30 Sept. 1994, X, B, 10, 13.

3. Cf. John H. Elliott, *A Home for the Homeless*, Philadelphia and London 1983; P.A. de Souza Nogueria, *O evangelho dos sem teto – Uma leitura da primeira carta de Pedro*, São Paulo 1993.

Pilgrimage to Wholeness:
An Image of Christian Life

Paul J. Philibert

In the first days of the fourteenth century, Dante Alighieri wrote these immortal lines:

> In the middle of the journey of our life
> I came to my senses in a dark forest
> for I had lost the straight path.[1]

Perhaps no writing in Western literature has captured the theme of spiritual pilgrimage as powerfully as these opening lines of the *Comedy*. The author of this immortal work was an exile on a pilgrimage to find a home and to understand the world. Political enemies had accused him of corruption, fined him, confiscated his goods, and sentenced him to be burned to death. In the *Divine Comedy* he has written the story of a journey of purification taking the anguished poet to another world through spheres of punishment, purification, and everlasting bliss.[2]

He claimed that his hope was to free from their misery people who are caught in the conflicts of the world by leading them to a state of beatitude. What Dante has done, at least, is to evoke a universal experience that everyone suffers at some time: losing one's bearings and meaning. This experience of *anomie* comes about through the loss of relational and environmental supports – the death of friends or the absence of work. In carrying the reader with him on a journey through the *Inferno* (the infernal site of punishment and awakening to remorse), the *Purgatorio* (the realm of purification), and into the 'delightful mountain' of the *Paradiso* (the realm of everlasting bliss), Dante invites readers to surmount the obstacles to happiness and move as pilgrims toward the fullness of life. Both his conviction that life is a journey and his evocation of the goal of life as beatitude with God anticipate and mirror the classical structure of many other accounts of the human journey as a pilgrimage.

Following Dante, I wish to indicate aspects of human development through the life cycle as a pilgrimage to wholeness. The underlying theme of this pilgrimage is the transition from *heteronomy* to *autonomy*. This is a movement from dependency to responsibility. The goal of life is to incarnate and manifest through the gestures of work and community the spiritual depths of a soul living in loving relation to its divine Source. The Johannine theme of a 'word made flesh' applies not only to the Christ, but to all who come to hear the voice of the Father. At the root of the theme of pilgrimage is a spiritual anthropology whose dynamic can be destroyed by a life lived exclusively in passive dependence upon the directive authority of others. In acknowledging that a mature life witnesses to spiritual convictions, we can also envisage the theme of 'flesh made word', that is, one's quality of presence and integrity being manifest in every aspect of life.

Every age has had the problem of bringing people to accept a creative responsibility for their own well-being and their mutual responsibility for community. Today, we see this played out on the world scene in the politics of nationalism, where authoritarian leaders have projected on to people caught in political struggles (as in Bosnia, Iran, Iraq, and elsewhere) a destructive compulsion to destroy one another in the interests of their leaders' self-promotion. Likewise, in the church, some eminent leaders have played upon the theme of dependency as a way of discouraging the continuation of a renewal ecclesiology. One of the great legacies of the Second Vatican Council is its call to moral and spiritual autonomy setting aside an older ecclesiology that would have reserved holiness to the few (see LG 40) or denied apostolic witness to the ecclesiastical non-professional (see LG 32–3). The evolution of spiritual personality in height, breadth and depth is one of the pressing issues for the re-launching of the pastoral renewal of the Council.

The development of the pilgrimage theme will be explored here in terms of three aspects of the human journey, called here 'the journey inward', 'the developmental journey', and 'the journey outward'. First, however, I will remark upon some biblical foundations for this theme as a theological project.

Biblical insights

The New Testament makes it very clear that the experience of meeting

Jesus is an invitation to significant transformation. The summons from the Lord is 'Follow me' (see Matt. 8.22; Mark 2.14; Luke 5.27; John 21.19,22). The spiritual journey for Christians is to follow Christ himself in a discipleship that involves imitation, intimacy, and identification.

In other passages, Jesus says 'I am the way, and the truth, and the life. No one comes to the Father except through me' (John 14.6). What is so often overlooked in this familiar passage is the goal; the believer is invited to come to the Father through the experience of knowing and loving Jesus. So similarly Jesus says 'I am the gate for the sheep' (John 10.8). Whoever enters into the community of oneness with the Father in Jesus is 'saved'. The sheepfold is a metaphor for a new life. The need for conversion is at the heart of the call to follow and to enter. This is at the core of the spiritual journey of the believer. Conversion implies change; change implies movement; movement evokes pilgrimage in this context.

In John's Gospel, the mystery of salvation is portrayed with the journey of Jesus as the Son who comes from the Father into this world. His journey back to the Father from this world through death and resurrection is the paradigm for our passage or passover following Jesus: 'I came from the Father and have come into the world; again, I am leaving the world and am going to the Father' (John 16.28). True life will be experienced by participating in this passover of Christ. One enters this mystery by responding to the Son of God through faith.

In a similar way, Paul's theology describes redemption in terms of the Son's journey as a passage of *kenosis* – the self-emptying of the divine Son that leads to his 'obedience unto death' and his exaltation into glory as the source of salvation for all (Phil. 2.5–11). This is the core of the Paschal mystery that delivers believers from slavery to sin into new life in the Spirit. Vatican II's Decree on Revelation speaks of Jesus perfecting revelation 'by fulfilling it through his whole work of making himself present and manifesting himself' (DV 4). Jesus is the transformer of the human journey not only by working wonders but in his very person and presence. But how does one arrive at a transforming relation with this Son who is the Way? The pilgrimage through the three journeys is one answer to this question.

In the third century, the school of Alexandria was influenced by themes of Neoplatonic philosophy that imagined the ascent of the soul from purgation through a life of virtue reaching to union and absorption with the One. Origen, one of the greatest seminal influences in Christian spirituality, described successive stages of spiritual progress. His description of a journey in three parts describes progress in the spiritual life for those he calls beginners, proficients and the perfect. This became one of the classical statements about typical moments in the spiritual journey. Following Origen, subsequent theologians repeatedly described the three ways of the spiritual life as the purgative, the illuminative and the unitive ways. This description of spiritual development parallels the theological imagination revealed in the medieval *summa* of Aquinas, who thought of the human agent on a journey of *exitus* and *reditus* (a coming forth from God the Creator in a journey that would ultimately lead back to God as Destiny).[3]

The journey inward

The goal of the 'inward journey' is to seek intimacy with God through contemplation and mystical surrender. One of the best known statements of this analogy of spiritual journey is found in Teresa of Avila's *The Interior Castle*. Teresa's image is that of a soul making a journey to different rooms in the castle of one's spiritual life. At the start, the pilgrim is in a state of grace, even if still attached to the pleasures of life and overpowered by self-will. The disciplines of spiritual practice (prayer, spiritual reading and obedience) tutor one in a life of virtue and sacrificing love. Gradually one moves to deeper prayer – the prayer of quiet – leading one to rest in God's love through desire. In time, someone willing to continue the journey towards the deeper prayer of union will pass into this divine intimacy through suffering passive purifications. Finally, what Teresa calls 'spiritual marriage' may occur as a state of union with God in the centre of the soul (its most interior space – 'the unitive way').[4]

The work of the 'journey inward' is something that constitutes a goal of spiritual transformation for every Christian in one form or another. On this journey, one learns dynamic silence. This means a pre-reflective awareness of the fullness of reality beyond words' capacity to symbolize. Connected with meditative disciplines such as the control of breathing, the loving repetition of a *mantra* that calls upon the Holy, or visualization exercises that lead one to bring the mind to be present in all the various parts of the body, dynamic silence is a kind of natural revelation of the great mystery of the gift of life. It is a door to the mystery of God's self-gift at the centre of life.

One aspect of this powerful experience of silence is what may be called 'incarnate contemplation', the realization that it is not only the discourse of thoughts and words in the mind that is the stuff of prayer, but the whole experienced phenomenal reality of the person. This quieting and opening of the psychological and spiritual experience of the person disposes one for the properly divine work of the grace of prayer. Prayer comes to be understood as more interior and totalizing within the Christian's experience of life. This is the way inward, preparing a person for the gift of God which takes place in 'sighs too deep for words' (Rom. 8.26).[5]

An important aspect of the journey inward is articulated in paragraph 16 of the Constitution on the Church in the Modern World. There we read:

> All have in their hearts a law written by God. To obey it is the very dignity of the human person; according to it the person will be judged . . . Conscience is the most secret core and sanctuary of a person. There one is alone with God, whose voice echoes in one's depths.

This teaching of Vatican II on maturity of conscience presupposes the development of a graced autonomy. Sensitivity to the voice of God in the depths of one's being presupposes the evolution of a responsiveness to the dynamics of inwardness. This inwardness is constituted by wonder, reflection, contemplation and surrender to intimacy with the God who reveals. How could there be a fully functional Christian life without growth in this dimension of the Christian pilgrimage?

The developmental journey

The fields of theology and spirituality are influenced by a dialogue with the empirical learnings of the social sciences, especially the science of psychology with its aspects of psychoanalytic theory, social psychology and transpersonal psychology. There is a growing popular awareness of human life as a journey marked by significant stages of development, passages, transitions, crises and marker events. Everyone is obliged to enter into the social world of adult functioning through gradual steps of awakening and co-operation. Roman Catholics have become familiar, particularly within religious education, with the concept of growth through stages. The writings of the psychologists Jean Piaget and Lawrence Kohlberg and the pastoral theologian James Fowler have become familiar to many even beyond North America.

Piaget concerned himself with growth towards an adequate human logic, while Kohlberg tried to develop a theory of growth towards adequate moral stages. Building upon the work of both of them, Fowler tried to describe transforming structures of human meaning in his 'stages of faith'.

In these works, there is a common trajectory of psychological transformation which underlies their accounts of human growth. To use Kohlberg's terms, each of us has the potential to move beyond an early childhood posture which is *pre-conventional*, that is, not yet in accord with adult meanings as they are taken for granted in our culture. This may mean the pre-logical fantasy of childhood thinking (Piaget), the self-centred bargaining of childhood morality (Kohlberg), or the naive and impressionable compliance of mythic-literal faith (Fowler). Everyone's journey to maturity begins in dependence upon the meaning and the understandings of more competent adults.[6]

Later we move into a *conventional* posture, one in which our understandings become more or less uniform with those of parents, teachers, school books, rules and laws, and historical traditions. We can call this 'operational thinking', 'a law-and-order morality', 'or a synthetic conventional faith'. Whatever we call it, the categories of the developmental journey make it clear that we can only arrive at such a posture gradually, through lots of testing and experimentation, and ultimately through social co-operation which brings us to need a world where trustworthy and taken-for-granted values can be spoken of, shared, and built upon.

Kohlberg and Fowler, moreover, lead us into a third position called the *post-conventional*. In this stage, something original, deep and restless leads us beyond the taken-for-granted. Kohlberg's account of a conscience orientation and Fowler's paradoxical faith and universal love stages (5 and 6) share the recognition that some adults are moved by an interior hunger for meaning which empowers them to set themselves over against the rigidity and neatness of a prefabricated social world.

Such developmental ideas are familiar. Whatever problems there may be with these accounts of the developmental journey, there is little doubt that each one of us must make a passage from dependence through co-operation to initiative like the journey portrayed in the stages of Piaget, Kohlberg and Fowler.

A feminist critique of stage theory

Given the importance of the movement from a pre-conventional through a conventional to a post-conventional understanding of society and morality, it is significant to look at a criticism of Kohlberg's stages of morality that came from a woman trained in the same psychological perspective as Kohlberg himself. Carol Gilligan published an important book entitled *In a Different Voice*, in which she claims that the descriptions of moral maturity proposed by Kohlberg are biased by male chauvinism.[7] Looking at Kohlberg's description of his post-conventional person in stages five and six, Gilligan finds that the mature person is described as being preoccupied with these values: the ideal, the abstract, the general or universal, and individualistic responsibility. Kohlberg portrays the stage-six person as a moral virtuoso who can stand against the crowd, who reasons his way into moral clarity, and who describes issues in broad, general and abstract terms. The highest stage goes to the person who is verbal, analytic and orientated on individual success.

Gilligan contrasts with this profile of male cognitive and moral values what she considers to be typical female values in our culture. Women whom she considers post-conventional in her studies of persons in moral crisis manifest a different set of values. In contrast to the men, these women tend to be preoccupied with the real rather than the ideal, the concrete rather than the abstract, the particular rather than the general, and the relational rather than the individualistic. Indeed, Gilligan's book arose out of her puzzlement at finding many of these women scored as stage-three moral thinkers by Kohlberg's associates. She came to realize that their insistence upon the importance of commitment, relation and enduring concern for the particularities of family and friendships led to these very values being assigned to a low stage of moral thinking because that is where, in Kohlberg's scheme, significant relational values are left behind.

Other indicators of inevitable transitions in logic, moral insight, and social thinking (that I have described here as the 'developmental journey') exist. For the present, however, the important factor is to indicate the necessity of such developmental progress. By contrasting the formalism of Kohlberg's stages to the contextualism of Gilligan's, we are led to recognize that no one of these theoretical maps is adequate on its own. While still awaiting a magisterial synthesis of factors in moral and social maturation, we must do our best to describe the qualities that are the legacy of the developmental journey. These qualities are *autonomy* (taking responsibility for moral decision), *co-operation* (understanding community as the basic unit of moral analysis), *compassion* (situating one's moral compass within a framework of human solidarity), and *passion for the good* (understanding life as an opportunity to witness to the benignity of the Creator). These goals are reached only step by step. The developmental journey describes ways in which we make our pilgrimage towards wholeness and how we can assist others to continue the long and difficult passage toward this goal.

The journey outward

The last part of the twentieth century is characterized by a concrete sense of the solidarity of all humankind. Like it or not, our destinies are visibly linked through the issues of war and peace, the pollution or well-being of the planet, and the need for global co-operation for the promotion of human well-being. Each time people are called beyond the protective sphere of their originating culture, they are brought into a surprising awareness of different ways of being human. The full meaning of humanity cannot be found in any one race or culture, but rather in the full spectrum of cultural, racial, and linguistic diversity. One of the great breakthroughs of the Second Vatican Council was its articulation of respect for and openness to the various traditions of humanity.

In a much neglected teaching within the Declaration on Non-Christian Religions (2) we read:

> Thus in Hinduism people contemplate the divine mystery and express it through the limitless riches of myths and through searching philosophical inquiry. They seek release from the anguish of our condition through ascetical practices or deep meditation or a loving, trusting flight toward God . . . Buddhism in its multiple forms acknowledges the radical insufficiency of this shifting world. It teaches a path by which people, in a devout and confident spirit, can either reach a state of absolute freedom or attain supreme enlightenment by their own effort or by higher assistance . . . Likewise, other religions to be found everywhere strive variously to answer the restless searchings of the human heart by proposing 'ways', which consist of teachings, rules of life, and sacred ceremonies.

The Council's intent in this document was to foster openness and co-operation with the great religions of the world at a moment in history when the co-operation of all those who acknowledge the Transcendent is necessary for human peace and well-being. However, beyond that important motive, the Council's spirit of openness mirrors a growing awareness that the cross-over experience (of seeing one's own cultural and religious tradition from the perspective of another) is enriching and healing in a world where even the most noble traditions are in transition and frequently caught in pre-renewal rigidity. The cross-over experience represents dissatisfaction with conventional spirituality and ecclesiastical discipline and with moral formalism. Merton once wrote that the Western Christian's desire to learn the spirituality of the East 'is a symptom of

Western man's desperate need to recover spontaneity and depth in a world which his technological skill has made rigid, artificial, and spiritually void'.[8] The motive for crossing over is to recover an authentic awareness of the reality of the Infinite and to see the disciplines of one's own tradition through the lens of some other great moral or religious tradition.

The late American scholar Joseph Campbell devoted his life to the exploration of the 'journey outward'. He was fascinated by the parallels of spiritual experience across traditions. In an informal statement about his scholarly interests he said:

> You've got the same body, with the same organs and energies, that Cro-Magnon Man had thirty thousand years ago. Living a human life in New York City or living a human life in the caves, you go through the same stages at childbirth, coming to sexual maturity, transformation of the dependency of childhood into the responsibility of manhood or womanhood, marriage, then failure of the body, gradual loss of its powers, and death.[9]

Campbell was fascinated by the symbols used by peoples across cultures. These symbols, whether in Egyptian carvings, Polynesian masks or American Iroquois tent paintings, speak to the same problems.

> It's as though the same play were taken from one place to another, and at each place the local players put on local costumes and act the same old way . . . It is a *mysterium*, a mystery, *tremendum et fascinans*, tremendous, horrific, because it smashes all of your fixed notions of things, and at the same time utterly fascinating because it's of your own nature and being. When you start thinking about these things, about the inner mystery, inner life, the internal life, there aren't too many images for you to use. You begin, on your own, to have the images that are already present in some other system of thought.[10]

Campbell's insights were developed in classical fashion in his book *The Hero With A Thousand Faces*, in which he did a comparative study of the hero's journey as typified in the traditions of many cultures, ancient and contemporary.[11] The goal of the 'outward journey' is to render the pilgrim conscious of the vastness of human experience. All traditions try in one way or another to enable their devotees to awaken to this powerful realization of the immensity of spiritual experience.

One form of this spiritual wisdom that is becoming increasingly well known in the West is Buddhist discipline. Buddhism speaks of an awakening that is based upon an 'emptying' or 'opening' of the self. It links awareness of one's nothingness (a person is *no thing*) to the experience of compassion. As Chögyom Trungpa wrote,

> When you begin realizing nonexistence, then you can afford to be more compassionate, more giving. A problem is that usually we would like to hold on to our territory . . . Once we begin to fixate on that ground, we have no way to give. Understanding *Shunyata* (emptiness) means that we begin to realize that there is no ground to get, that we are ultimately free, non-aggressive, open . . . We have lots to gain and nothing to lose.[12]

Similarly, Thich Nhat Hanh speaks of compassion as rooted in awareness of suffering:

> We see the suffering caused by the destruction of life, and we vow to cultivate compassion and use it as a source of energy for the protection of people, animals, plants, and minerals . . . And not to kill is not enough. We must also learn ways to prevent others from killing . . . Life is so precious, yet in our daily lives we are usually carried away by our forgetfulness, anger, and worries . . . The best use of our time is being generous and really being present with others . . . We seem to take refuge in our work in order to avoid confronting our real sorrow and inner turmoil. We express our love and care for others by working hard, but if we do not have time for the people we love, if we cannot make ourselves available to them, how can we say that we love them?[13]

These words of Thich Nhat Hanh illustrate the way in which the wisdom of another tradition can warn us of the ways in which a careless living of our own tradition can ensnare us in destructive habits. The goal of the journey outward is not to adopt another's tradition, but to return home with a new awareness of the immensity of what is at stake in human living. The result is a better focus on the wealth of wisdom within our own tradition. Described this way, however, the 'journey outward' can appear to be esoteric, élitist, and reserved to a small minority of persons. In fact, everyone is invited to some form of the journey outward.

Compassion is the key to the door that opens on this path. Throughout the world today, there are new movements of volunteer service that allow persons to enter into an experience of the immensity of the beauty of existence through the discipline of loving service. The notable examples of *L'Arche*, the Missionaries of Charity (who incorporate so many temporary volunteers to serve among them), or the many national volunteer corps that offer structured opportunities for social service for young people in their countries are examples of the application of this principle. The fundamental point is that in coming to know the need of another through personal contact, one sees oneself in the suffering eyes of humanity. There is a powerful transformation that takes place in the experience of service, the conversion to compassion, that allows all life to be seen and experienced with new eyes.

The experience of pilgrimage

What all three of these journeys – the journey inward, the developmental journey, and the journey outward – have in common is a principle described by developmental psychologists as 'cognitive dissonance'.[14] At some point, our experience outstrips our understanding and we are forced to rework the philosophy and wisdom from which we operate. In the 'journey inward', this moment occurs when, in the course of growing intimacy with God, we reach the point where we recognize that God is more accepting of us than we are of ourselves. We discover this in the anointing of loving tenderness that grows within the path of dynamic silence. This is a revolutionary moment in which, for the first time, we really begin to understand the infinity of love.

In the 'developmental journey', the critical moment comes when we realize that the conventional structures of our social world are too rigid to be able to do justice to the extraordinary things that occur in anyone's life. What the ancient Greeks called *epikeia* is the gateway to the 'post-conventional'. Only through the discomfort of acknowledging the need to be autonomous – personally responsible in a creative way – does anyone accept finally that every tradition must be renewed. This is what generativity does in its preoccupation with the needs of others and the needs of the community.

In the 'journey outward', the critical moment comes when one discovers that 'wounds are not a waste' (see I Peter 2.24). By entering into the intimacy of compassionate love with the wounded, one begins to experience the ironic power of the 'wounded healer'.[15] At this point, we learn to accept the mystery that God is immanent to this world in all its cataclysms, loving of the weakest of persons, and empowering of the slightest gestures of compassion. 'Truly, I tell you, just as you did [this] to one of the least of these who are members of my family, you did it to me' (Matt. 25.40).

All these transformations are part of autonomy. What is clear now is that autonomy does not mean independence but interdependence. It is a call not to wilful isolation, but to willing compassion. It is only at the far end of these journeys that autonomy becomes embodied in wisdom, justice, and compassion. That is why the pilgrimage to wholeness, as described in this way, is essential for human integrity.

Dante was tempted to go back in the dark wood in order to flee from the fierce beasts that confronted him, hoping more than anything to return to the way things were before. This, of course, is always the temptation. Like Dante, we each need a Virgil (a mentor) to lead us on the difficult journey through our *Inferno* and our *Purgatorio* towards the mountain of bliss. Or perhaps it is better to say that we each are called to become a Virgil – a mentor. The journeys described here as aspects of our human pilgrimage to wholeness are not solitary adventures, but invitations to communion. Each one of these journeys awakens us to our solidarity with all our human companions on the pilgrimage to wholeness. We help one another to see and to persevere.

Notes

1. Dante Alighieri, *The Divine Comedy*, translated by H. R. Huse, New York 1954, 7.

2. See Joseph Gallagher, *To Hell and Back with Dante: A Lift for the Intimidated*, Ligouri, Missouri 1996.

3. See Aquinas, *Summa Theologiae*, Vol. 1, *Christian Theology*, ed. T. Gilby, New York 1963: Appendix I, 43f.

4. Teresa of Avila, *The Interior Castle*, London 1988. See J. Welch, *Spiritual Pilgrims: Carl Jung and Teresa of Avila*, New York 1982.

5. For our transitional age, there ought to be a 'Spiritual Bill of Rights' that would include: 1. the right of every Christian to be initiated into dynamic silence in order to learn that silence is a realm of many levels reaching all the way to the Infinite; 2. the right to learn about embodied contemplation as a dimension of witness to incarnate presence; 3. the right to be introduced into a spirituality of communion that offers spiritual solidarity with all human beings beyond the limiting dynamics of roles; and 4. the right to be called to the insight of compassion which links all persons beyond their social and religious identities.

6. J. Piaget, *The Moral Judgment of the Child*, translated by Marjorie Gabain, New York 1965; L. Kohlberg, *The Philosophy of Moral Development*, Vol. I: *Moral Stages and the Idea of Justice*, San Francisco 1981; J. Fowler, *Stages of Faith: The Psychology of Human Development and the Quest for Meaning*, San Francisco 1981.

7. Carol Gilligan, *In a Different Voice: Psychological Theory and Women's Development*, Cambridge, Mass. 1982.

8. T. Merton, *The Way of Chuang Tzu*, New York 1965, 16.

9. J. Campbell, *The Power of Myth*, New York 1988, 37–9.

10. Ibid., 38–9.

11. J. Campbell, *The Hero with a Thousand Faces*, New York 1949.

12. Chögyam Trungpa, *Training the Mind and Cultivating Loving Kindness*, Boston 1993, 11–17.

13. Thich Nhat Hanh, *Living Buddha, Living Christ*, New York 1995, 91–4.

14. All three developmentalists follow the interpretation that 'cognitive dissonance' brings about movement for stage development. A person's recognition that existing cognitive structures do not adequately mediate a satisfying picture of reality as it is coming to be known in new ways motivates the development of new structures for thinking. See Piaget on 'equilibration', e.g., in J. Phillips, Jr, *The Origins of Intellect: Piaget's Theory*, San Francisco 1969, ch. 1.

15. See H. Nouwen, *The Wounded Healer: Ministry in Contemporary Society*, New York 1972.

The 'Pilgrim Church' of Vatican II: A Tale of Two Altars

Alex García-Rivera

I. A semiotic approach

Studies of Vatican II ecclesiology often take a 'before' and 'after' approach. The church before Vatican II is contrasted with the church after the Council. This study will take a similar if not identical approach towards understanding a particular dimension of Vatican II ecclesiology – the 'pilgrim' church. Such an approach, however, carries the danger of over-emphasizing the differences at the risk of remaining silent about the continuity between the pre- and post-Vatican II church. One may be led to think that the notion of the 'pilgrim' church is an innovation by the Council. This study assumes that there is a continuous self-understanding by the church as a pilgrim community, even if such an understanding cannot be found explicitly in pre-Vatican II church documents. Indeed, the value of this study might be not in seeing the notion of the 'pilgrim' church as a 'new' ecclesiological development but as an ever-present reality of the church before and after the Council. The insight offered here is to look at the notion of the 'pilgrim' church not simply in terms of a reaction against an outdated notion of the church but also in terms of examining how the church might have seen itself as a 'pilgrim' before and after the council.

Such a task involves more than examining concepts and notions written in documents. Concepts and notions can also be expressed through signs and symbols 'written' not on paper but in the space and walls of the church itself. Such an approach not only involves a traditional analysis of written texts but also includes what is known as a semiotic analysis of 'cultural texts'. The semiotic analysis of non-traditional theological texts was first attempted by Virgil Elizondo (Elizondo, 1977). Robert Schreiter and Alex

García-Rivera subsequently developed a formal framework for Elizondo's pioneering study known as the *semiotics of culture*.

Semiotics *per se* studies signs and the relationships between signs. Signs, in the semiotics of culture, connect to one another by means of codes or rules which in 'creative collaboration' produce the messages in a culture. A linguistic metaphor for this process would be a sentence. If words are signs, and a meaningful sentence made of a string of these words a message, then the rules, the grammar, which strings together such words into that sentence are the codes. In a 'cultural text', then, one has signs instead of words, codes instead of grammar, and messages instead of sentences. The task of a semiotic analysis of culture is 'reading' the cultural text, which means locating 'its signs, the codes that place the signs in dynamic interaction, and the messages that are conveyed' (Schreiter, 1985; García-Rivera, 1995a). The use of the semiotics of culture approach allows the tracing of continuities of thought even if they are not written down. By using the 'before' and 'after' approach together with the 'semiotics of culture' approach, both the uniqueness and continuity of Vatican II's notion of the 'pilgrim' church are given their due. Furthermore, by preserving both the uniqueness and continuity of the notion of the 'pilgrim' church, a fresh insight into the nature of the church may take place. This study begins, then, with a look at a non-traditional 'text', a church building full of tradition – a cathedral.

II. The first altar

The cathedral of Metz stood before me filled with tradition and rich with symbols. I had come to the Alsace-Lorraine region in France to give a paper on the Latin American church. My gracious hosts from the University of Metz had arranged a visit to this famous cathedral. Now, the massive and unmoving walls of this ancient ancestor of the Latin American church rose before me and affirmed my suspicions of pre-Vatican II ecclesiology. The essence of the pre-Vatican II church must have looked like this – a fortress under siege with stone walls rising to the heavens dividing earthly space into an outside and an inside. Or so my first impression ran. When I walked inside the cathedral, this impression was transformed. On these massive walls, huge areas of stone had been cut out and, in their place, dancing areas of colour and light woven together with delicate threads of lead stood, or rather, blurred an impregnable divide – the one between heaven and earth. These walls had been meant not to create boundaries but to blur them!

I began to pay more attention to the intrinsic logic of this place. The cathedral docent pointed out the differences between these vibrant visions of light. Indeed, one could see drastic differences in style. Next to each other stood windows done in a Gothic style, severe and restrained, and windows done in the manner of the Renaissance, full of colour and life. And, over on the corner, a window from this century built by Marc Chagall invited us to participate in its surreal mysticism. Within my breast a new understanding began to emerge, but I could not name it. Then I turned my head and saw a name, actually, initials rather than a name, carved upon the wall next to me. A date (1529) had been carved next to them. Understanding, now, began to take form. Metz cathedral had been on a journey. The cathedral building showed on its walls and windows the signs of a journey through diverse eras and of being host to a multitude of travellers. Where, however, were these travellers journeying? What had been their motivation? The windows appeared to be significant. They suggested that these travellers had been journeying to a vision imagined by faith. But how does one travel to a vision? How does one travel to an imagination?

As I looked around, I saw another sign. Two altars stood in sharp contrast to each other. One altar pressed against the cathedral's eastern wall. A priest celebrating mass at this altar would have disappeared into the cavernous space created by the walls and windows of the cathedral. The altar collaborated with the entire logic of the cathedral space to emphasize the blurring of the boundary between earth and heaven. Indeed, this altar looked like a gateway. Those who celebrated at its foot were lost sight of as if they had entered a door opening into another space. The altar marked a dimension of pre-Vatican II ecclesiology that I had not understood before. The cathedral of Metz appeared to be more than a way station for travellers travelling towards a vision of faith. At its east end stood an altar, a type of door, which offered the weary traveller an entrance opening up a view of the journey's end. Thus, the cathedral of Metz was not only a way station but also an entrance to the vision of these weary travellers. The altar of the pre-Vatican II cathedral of Metz was the key to its religious imagination, to its vision of faith. It was a door to a view. This was, however, a very special kind of view. It emphasized a heaven come to earth which, in its transcendence, was apparently also a refreshment. The travellers of pre-Vatican II Metz had been pilgrims motivated by a transcendent vision of things to come, yet refreshed by its immanence at a 'door' located at its eastern wall.

III. The second altar

In contrast, the other altar stood out from the wall, thrusting itself into the space and demanding a presence for itself. At Metz, this altar occupied the exact place where the horizontal 'arms' of the cathedral's width intersected with its 'body's' length. In other words, the altar had now moved from the 'head' to the 'heart' of the cathedral. This was the altar of Vatican II. A priest celebrating mass at this altar could not be ignored. The Vatican II mass, however, as practised in many parishes, sees little of the priest at the altar. Readers, eucharistic ministers, altar boys and girls, guest preachers and parish announcements all share the altar with the priest. Moreover, the altar itself is surrounded by the assembly of faithful. As in the pre-Vatican II altar, the priest disappears; this time, however, not into the 'material' space of the cathedral but into the 'human' space of the parish. In other words, the priest disappears into the 'heart' of the cathedral, and now a new type of door is revealed. It is the nature of this 'door' that concerns this study.

That such a door may be found at the 'heart' of the cathedral rather than at its 'head' may not surprise those familiar with the theology of John XXIII. His theology may be summarized in a phrase taken from a speech given shortly after his election as Pope: *veritatem facere in caritate*, 'to do truth in charity'. Next to the vertical dimension of defending the truth of Catholic doctrine, John XXIII affirmed, the episcopal ministry includes a horizontal dimension opened up through the exercise of charity (Descalzo, 1967, 31). For John XXIII, the heights of Christian truth were measured not by the eye but by the heart. The height of the church's dogmatic concern for heaven joins with the breadth of the church's pastoral concern for the earth. Their intersection, like the stained-glass windows of the pre-Vatican II church, effects a blurring of heaven and earth but in a different manner.

IV. The pilgrim church and Vatican II

This difference is evident in the changes to key concepts between the first and last draft of *Lumen Gentium*. Two years before the first meeting, Pope John asked his episcopate from all over the world what should be the programme of the council. He received a total of 8972 proposals filling 9420 pages (Vorgrimler, 1967, 106). This vast amount of material was assigned to the commission *De doctrina fidei et morum* headed by Cardinal Ottaviani. The commission had been assigned the immense task of picking out the doctrinal themes for a dogmatic treatment of the church, *De Ecclesia*. These themes would be discussed at the Council. Ottaviani's commission worked the next two years completing an initial draft consisting of 11 chapters and an appendix on Mary. The first chapter of this initial draft was entitled 'The nature of the church militant'. By the time of the last draft, the language of the 'militant' church had changed to the language of the 'pilgrim' church.

The change from the 'militant' to the 'pilgrim' church took place through a new solution of the relationship between the spiritual and the temporal, i.e. between the 'two powers'. The traditional relationship had been forged in the struggle of the church (led by the Popes) against the absolute claims made by secular powers. In other words, the church was increasingly seen after the eleventh century as a *societas perfectas*. With respect to the temporal power of the church, this means that the church has of itself every means by which to achieve its end. This meaning emphasizes the visible nature of the church through its juridical order (Congar, 1986, 138). With respect to the spiritual power of the church, this means that the church enjoys a *libertas Ecclesiae* which makes certain demands on its structure. This meaning emphasizes the invisible nature of the church through the charisms and dynamism of its members. The 'militant' church had come to the Council in terms of a visible, juridical society justified in organizing itself over and against the claims of worldly powers by virtue of its claims to a special type of liberty.

Between this first formulation and the last draft, the second, spiritual meaning of *societas perfectas*, the *libertas Ecclesiae*, took on a deeper sense. The liberty of the Spirit which animated the church was not so much a militant defiance against the world as a freedom to embrace it. This charitable sense of the *libertas Ecclesiae* began to perfuse and penetrate this first offer of a visible, temporal 'militant' church. The result was a more profound sense of the *societas perfecta*. The church was beginning to be seen as a society made up of both a temporal reality with visible borders distinguishing the church and an invisible, spiritual reality extended beyond those visible borders embracing the whole world. In other words, the 'militant' church had become transformed from a society on the march in defiance of the world to a communion in pilgrimage inviting the world to join.

Indeed, one of the key ecclesiological concepts to be given new depth was the notion of the church as a society to the church as a communion. The church, of course, is a society. It is, in one sense of the term, a visible body of institutions organized through its laws into a moral solidarity. Yet this sense of the term leaves much to be desired. The church is not simply a society of the visible but also a society of the invisible. The emphasis on the visibility of the church was understandable as a way of correcting an overemphasis on the invisibility of the church by the Reformation churches. By the time of Vatican II, however, a different world from that of the Reformation and Counter-Reformation offered new challenges. The emphases which had given identity and direction to the church in the sixteenth century began to lose their force in the twentieth. The world, in fact, had become more materialistic. If an emphasis on the visible had been an ally to the church in past centuries, now it was a liability. Pius XII addressed this imbalance with his encyclical *Mystici Corporis*. To a world which stressed the material and the visible, Pius XII presented a vision of the church as a visible institution living an invisible reality, a divine communion with its Lord. Yet, for the bishops and cardinals gathered for the Second Council, even such a powerful image did not fully rise to the profound challenge presented by a post-World War II world.

A majority of bishops and cardinals, in fact, were in agreement over the first draft. The nature of the church as a community should be stressed over that of the church as a society. Bishop Elchinger, for example, noted that earlier the church had been known above all as an institution, but now the church must be known as a community. Cardinal Liénart went further. He regretted that the visible church and the mystical body of Christ had been too closely associated (Vorgrimler, 1967, 108). By the time of the last draft, a magnificent transformation took place. The universal church is revealed as a 'people brought into unity from the unity of the Father, the Son, and the Holy Spirit' (*Lumen Gentium*, 4). In other words, the church 'grows visible through the power of God in the world' (LG, 3). The cosmic authority of the Father and the expansive liberty of the Spirit gave dimension and depth to a church gathered in the Son's name. The mystical body of Pius XII now extended beyond the visible boundaries of its institutions.

Perhaps the most telling dimension given to this sense of the church as community is the crucial emphasis given to the relationship between the Johannine and Pauline ecclesial traditions. Jesus' words to his mother and the 'beloved disciple' from the cross – 'Woman, here is your son, . . . here is your mother' – may be seen as paradigmatic of this communion. Not Pentecost but the cross takes emphasis here. As such, the cross may be seen as the origin and growth of the church symbolized by the water and blood flowing from the wound given the crucified Jesus (LG, 3). Indeed, the council appears to see the borders of the church through the eyes of the crucified Christ – 'And I, if I be lifted up from the earth, will draw all men to myself' (John 12.32; LG, 3). Thus, through this 'lifting up', 'Christ, our Pasch, is sacrificed' (I Cor. 5.7) in the sacrament of the eucharist, expressing not only the visible unity of believers (1 Cor. 10.17) but also calling all people to union with Christ, the *lumen gentium*.

These relationships, in a sense, summarize the modern journey of the notion of the church as society to the church as communion. The mystical communion called the body of Christ is also a sign and sacrament of the *lumen gentium*. The body of Christ, then, turns out to be more than an analogy, i.e. a static perception through metaphorical comparison between two dissimilar things. Although it is that. The Body of Christ now also becomes an *anagogy*, a dynamic perception that transforms and 'lifts up'. As anagogy, the body of Christ becomes a sacrament, an efficacious visible sign of an invisible reality, a healing of the wounds of the world symbolized by the water and blood flowing from the wounds of the crucified Christ. This community known as the body of Christ is at once a humble and magnificent vision of the church. It is humble because its visible origins lie at the humiliation of its crucified Christ. It is magnificent because it partakes of an invisible reality of glorious dimensions.

A second ecclesiological concept which took new depth at the council was the holiness of the church. The sanctification of the human being when seen through juridical eyes becomes, in a limited sense, a simple analogy with the society of heaven. To be holy, the human being of the present times must visibly live a life analogous to the life he or she will lead in the end times. Such an analogy was found to be deficient and one-sided at the council. Holy life in the present time is more than a temporal analogy to life in heaven. That is, holiness now is analogous to holiness then. Holy life in the present time is also more than a spiritual analogy. These analogies are in themselves helpful. Analogical language helps us to understand the distinctiveness of the temporal and the spiritual dimensions of the church's holiness. Nonetheless, the council wanted to stress the indivisibility of the temporal and spiritual dimensions as they apply to the holiness of the church and thus to the sanctification of the human being.

This required more than an analogical language aimed at understanding a view of life; it required an anagogical language aimed at transforming a way of life. Sanctification, after all, is about *metanoia*, conversion to a holy way of life. Anagogical language is, in a sense, the language of sanctification, the language of grace and redemption. It motivates rather than understands, 'lifts up' rather than 'lifts out'. It aims for a vision that transforms. Such an understanding of holiness must have as a corollary a corresponding view of human nature. This view must include two components. First, the capacity of the human being for holiness must be affirmed without denying the tragic reality of sin. Second, the dynamism of human nature needs to be articulated and clarified over a one-sided view of human nature as strictly an eternal and unchanging essence. The Council accomplished both by clarifying the relationship of the church of the present times to the kingdom of the end times.

The church, the Council affirmed, is not the kingdom of God, but the kingdom of God subsists in the church. Such a relationship may be seen as anagogical. The kingdom of the end times 'lifts up' the church of the present times, making her not only a visible but also an efficacious sign of a profound invisible reality. Since both the church and the world will share in the end times, the church by faithfully living in the present times becomes redemptive not only for her visible institutions but for the entire world. The church, by faithfully living in the present times, not only graces her members but all human beings. In other words, through its anagogical relationship to the end time, the church of the present time becomes a sacrament to the world.

This anagogical relationship is also reflected in the council's exalted view of humanity. Human beings possess a special dignity among all other creatures. They are made in the image of God (*Gaudium et Spes*, 1). As such, human beings, like the church, also have a relationship to the kingdom of God. Human beings, whether members of the church or not, also relate to the end time. This relationship may be expressed as the dignity of the human being. The human being as an image of God is more than an analogy to God which helps us understand the nature of our humanity by 'lifting out' the human being from other creatures. The human being as an image of God is, as well, an anagogy to God which 'lifts up' human being as having certain dignity. This 'lifting up' clarifies what in the Reformation became a paradoxical view of the human being as both sinner and justified. The dignity of the human being as an anagogical relationship to the end time reveals at once not only the need of the human being for redemption but also his and her capacity for grace. This is more than the paradoxical coincidence of opposites; it is a true anagogy. Human beings are effectively sanctified through grace. Holiness in the present times is an actual reality, if also a constant need, because there is an effective relationship between the end time and the present.

V. The significance of the second altar

Thus two crucial ecclesiological concepts were given depth and new dimensions at the Second Vatican Council: the church as society and the church as holy. The notion of the church as a holy society was deepened into the notion of the church as a community growing in holiness through its spiritual and temporal relationship to the end time. This, I would like to suggest, is the understanding of the church which the Vatican Council calls the 'pilgrim church'. Such an understanding, at least, is as far as the 'written' documents take us. I believe, however, there is more. Let me suggest that another dimension of the notion of the 'pilgrim church' exists. This extra dimension may be revealed through continuing the semiotic reflection started at the beginning of this study. This continuation centres on the significance of the second altar, the altar of Vatican II. The second altar, in the semiotics of culture, becomes another 'document', a 'text' which has something to say about the 'pilgrim church'. The following discussion is an attempt to understand the significance of this unwritten 'text' and what it may tell us about the nature of the 'pilgrim church'.

The altar of the post-Vatican II church takes on special significance for an understanding of Vatican II ecclesiology. Of all the changes that took place after the Second Council, the altar is the most visible manifestation of the Council's presence. Most Roman Catholic churches built before the Second Council now contain two altars. Going back to our example of the cathedral of Metz, one may note that the post-Vatican II altar has a similar semiotic function to the pre-Vatican II altar. Both act towards the 'blurring' of heaven and earth as an entrance to a vision. For the post-Vatican II altar this takes place not so much through the inert space of the cathedral but through the 'human' space gathered around the altar. It is here, I believe, that the 'pilgrim' church is to be found. The nature of the 'pilgrim' church is tied up in the nature of this 'human' space.

The written documents describe this 'human' space as a community. A popular notion of community sees a harmonious, intimate group of people having a great deal in common. This notion of community, however, does not appear to describe the 'human' space defined by a 'pilgrim' people. A 'pilgrim' community is hardly one that has a great deal in common. Pilgrims, by definition, are 'outsiders'. They come from 'other' communities as 'strangers' to be with other 'strangers', each journeying for their own special reason, their own special circumstance. What they have in common is the end of the journey and the journey itself. A 'human' space which is also a 'pilgrim' church must therefore include these two elements of the 'pilgrim' experience. The 'human' space, then, gathered around the altar describes not so much a 'door' opening a view of heaven as a 'heart' which is at the same time a journey to and a vision of heaven. The 'human' space gathered around the 'heart' of the cathedral is a dynamic beholding, a beating 'heart', a vision of the end times which turns out to be a journeying.

The 'human' space that is a 'pilgrim' church, then, is more than a gathering of people having a common vision. It is a dynamic envisioning of an end yearned for in common. This 'human' space, then, is akin to the imagination. The imagination, unfortunately, is associated with fantasies or dreams. The envisioning at the foot of the altar, however, is more than a fantasy or a dream. The envisioning at the foot of the altar is sacramental. It is an envisioning of an invisible reality, and in its envisioning one is transformed, changed, sanctified. Thus the dynamic envisioning around the altar is grounded not on a collective fantasy but on an invisible reality which takes flesh within this 'human' space. This suggests that the imagination of the 'pilgrim' church is more than a psychology, an act of the mind. It is, rather, an anthropology, an act of the entire human being, individual and social. Such analysis suggests that to an exalted view of the human being as the image of God there corresponds an exalted view of the human imagination. Human ability to envision is at the heart of a 'pilgrim church' that is a sacrament, that has the capacity not only to perceive an invisible reality but also for an effective relationship to that reality. Human ability to envision is at the heart of a 'pilgrim church' that has the capacity not only to perceive the kingdom of God in its midst but also to be related to this kingdom in a real and effective way.

Furthermore, the arrangement of the second altar at the cathedral of Metz suggests that the locus for such envisioning is not the 'head' but the 'heart'. The human 'space' around the post-Vatican II altar is, in a sense, a 'heart' that envisions. This sense has strong biblical roots. The heart also happens to be a biblical locus for the imagination (Kearney, 1988). Furthermore, the biblical sense of the imagination appears to be more than a mental affair (García-Rivera, 1995b). Indeed, an imagination that is a psychology involves an envisioning that is private. Such an envisioning would be kept within church walls. An imagination, however, that is an anthropology involves an envisioning that is public and meant to be seen beyond church walls. Thus, the intent of the Johannine ecclesiology is given a means by which to take flesh. Through the anthropological imagination of the 'pilgrim church' our Lord is lifted up for all the world to 'see'. Through the anthropological imagination, the world is also invited to envision an invisible reality within its midst. As such, the imagination of the 'pilgrim church' is not a private but a public vision of that which gives life to the world but the world does not perceive, the 'heart' of the world, its Lord, Jesus Christ. Such an envisioning is meant, as the crucified Christ of John's Gospel meant, to 'draw all men to myself'.

The second altar, then, happens to be more than the 'heart' of a church; it is the 'heart' of the world. Thus, the Vatican II notion of the 'pilgrim church' may be seen to possess another dimension through this unwritten 'text'. The pilgrimage to the end time takes place not simply on the road, nor simply through the times, but in the heart. Around the second altar, a journey through an invisible reality takes place through a 'human' space, the heart, and, in the journey, a vision takes form that transforms not simply all gathered but the entire world outside church walls. For the 'pilgrim church' gathered around the second altar has actually gathered around the 'heart' of the world and, through their journey of the anthropological imagination, its members have also brought the world along with them.

VI. Conclusion

The Second Vatican Council set out to articulate a vibrant ecclesiology. Through the notion of the 'pilgrim church' they not only succeeded but may also have laid the foundations for a vibrant anthropology. The anthropology suggested in this study is the anthropological imagination, the journey of the 'pilgrim' church at the 'heart' of the world, sanctifying not only the pilgrim but the world as well. As such, this study has been a tale of two altars. One altar took us to the gates of heaven, the other to the 'heart' of the world. Their distinctiveness helps understanding one in terms of the other. Together, however, they also contribute to another, perhaps deeper, understanding. Heaven and earth are intrinsically connected. The 'gates' of heaven are to be found at the 'heart' of the world. We who are in pilgrimage to those gates have learned from the Second Vatican Council that the yearning for the end times is not a yearning for the end of the world but, rather, for its heart.

Bibliography

Yves Congar, OP, 1986: 'Moving Towards a Pilgrim Church', in *Vatican II Revisited: By Those Who Were There*, ed. Alberic Stacpoole, 129–52, Minneapolis.
Jose Luis Martin Descalzo, 1967: *El Concilio de Juan y Pablo: Documentos*

Pontificios Sobre la Preparación, Desarollo e Interpretación del Vaticano II, Biblioteca de Autores Christianos, Madrid.

Virgil Elizondo, 1977: 'Our Lady of Guadalupe as a Cultural Symbol', in *Liturgy and Cultural Traditions*, 25–33, New York.

Alex García-Rivera, 1995a: *St Martin de Porres: The 'Little Stories' and the Semiotics of Culture*, Faith and Cultures, Maryknoll.

———, 1995b, 'A Matter of Presence', *Journal of Hispanic/Latino Theology* 3 (November).

Richard Kearney, 1988: 'The Hebraic Imagination', in *The Wake of Imagination: Toward a Postmodern Culture*, Minneapolis.

Robert Schreiter, 1985: *Constructing Local Theologies*, Maryknoll and London.

Herbert Vorgrimler (ed.), 1967: *Commentary on the Documents of Vatican II*.

III · Pastoral Practice

Pastoral Opportunities of Pilgrimages

Virgil Elizondo

Pilgrimage is one of the oldest physical-spiritual exercises of humanity and of our Christian tradition. It can certainly have many different meanings and functions for different persons, yet the phenomenon of pilgrimage appears as a constant in humanity regardless of the many changes in the human condition. In speaking to the convocation of pilgrimage directors in 1980, John Paul II stated: 'You have in your hands a key to the religious future of our times.'

Pilgrimages are not of the essence of Christian faith, but they can definitely be privileged moments in everyone's personal journey of faith, as well as fascinating adventures full of unsuspected experiences. One does not have to go on a geographical pilgrimage to grow in the faith, but a true pilgrimage can certainly help to advance one's personal faith-journey to the fullness of life. An authentic pilgrimage will be a privileged time and space for discovery, discernment, healing and illumination. The church has a marvellous opportunity for helping to make these deeply personal moments of life's journey even more fruitful than they would be even without the presence of the church.[1] People want to go on pilgrimage. How can the church be of genuine service in the pilgrim's quest?

Because people come in great numbers and the majority of them come in a spirit of searching, repentance, gratitude and openness to divine favour, pilgrimage sites become privileged places of evangelization and pastoral ministry. Throughout the pilgrimage, the church will have many opportunities of evangelizing through hospitality, conversation and various forms of pastoral ministry. The pilgrimage itself is as important as the experience at the sacred site itself, or maybe even more important. One cannot rush a pilgrimage and expect to obtain its beneficial effects. A sufficient length of time is crucial to an authentic experience of pilgrimage.

Sweat, struggle, fatigue and even blistered feet could well be important elements of a pilgrimage.

On the pilgrimage route and during the extended time spent at the sacred site, one has the opportunity, like Jesus with the disciples on the road to Emmaus, to converse freely with strangers about what is happening in one's life, society and the world, to discuss openly what is in one's heart and to reflect on the meaning of the scriptures in the light of the events of life. In the word of the stranger who is simply a fellow traveller, we can easily hear the most precious 'word of God' that we will ever hear in our lives. No one programmes, directs or manipulates their conversation, so all are completely given to the guidance of the spirit. This is invitational, story-sharing and dialogical evangelization at its best! Not proselytistic, moralistic or doctrinal jargon, but the incarnational language of life, the story-telling language of the gospel. It is in this very context that we, the pilgrims, become 'word of God' to one another without even realizing it. At the very moment it is happening we may not think of it as 'word of God', but in reflection, some very ordinary phrases, words, images and insights will definitely emerge as God's word to me at this particular moment of my life.

The pastoral ministry of the church in regard to pilgrimages might be divided into three areas.

I. Preparation for the pilgrimage

One of the core images of the church used by Vatican II and called forth frequently by the third eucharistic prayer is that of the pilgrim church. The very pilgrimage itself reflects and is a living experience of the innermost reality of the church. Hence it would be good if parishes, dioceses, religious, seminaries and universities would encourage their people to go on pilgrimage some time in their lives. But it should be clear from the beginning that 'a pilgrimage' is not just a religious term for modern-day tourism.

The preparation for the pilgrimage should not be merely on the material level, but even more so on the spiritual one. Regardless of the immediate reason why a person decides to go on a pilgrimage, the pilgrim should be helped to look forward to the entire process as a privileged time in his/her life – a time of unsuspected and uncontrolled life-giving surprises. The pilgrimage should be a fabulous journey of discovery – of self, others, other cultures, nature and God. It will be a time of inner freedom from daily affairs and pressures which will thus allow us to see, hear, remember, comprehend and talk about aspects of life which have previously remained unnoticed. Those going on the pilgrimage must be ready really to leave behind their business, professional and family concerns – no faxes, e-mail or telephone calls. It is crucial to 'let oneself go' in order to be disposed to the action of God during the pilgrimage.

In the context of spiritual freedom from ordinary concerns, one can more easily come to grips with both the shadow and the luminous sides of one's life and accept, respect and love oneself as one truly is. One should not go on the pilgrimage with well-defined expectations, but rather with an open mind and heart, to discover and obtain insight and favours which are beyond the control of any earthly authority. It is in the spirit of total openness and surrender to the wisdom and power of divine love that the fullest benefits of the pilgrimage will be obtained. The spirituality of pilgrimage, that is, the spirituality of the inner freedom that comes through distance and detachment, is fundamental for a truly successful pilgrimage.

Prayer is always answered, but not always in the way we think. It is true that many people go on a pilgrimage seeking a special favour, especially a physical cure, and there is nothing wrong with this, as it is evident that it is not the magic of any one place but the faith of the pilgrim which brings about healing. As Jesus often stated: 'Your faith has healed you.' As God has manifested very special and visible favours in certain places on earth, it is obvious that going to such a place can certainly intensify the faith of the pilgrim, the faith which can move mountains and restore life. Miracles do take place, many more than we dare to suspect, but quite often the greater number of miracles does not bring the physical healing of a person, but the inner healing of the entire person who through the process of the pilgrimage discovers a new life. Often it is the healing which comes through a new vision and appreciation of life that is a result of insight obtained during the pilgrimage. I have had many testimonies of such experiences.

II. Pastoral ministry during the pilgrimage

Pastoral ministry among those who embark on pilgrimage on their own

Whereas many people go on pilgrimage groups, some choose to start on pilgrimage alone. Yet in the very process of the journey, others will be met and new friendships will be formed. Whether one is on a pilgrimage to a sanctuary, to a monastery, to a mountain, to the desert or to some other special place, the church can be of assistance whenever possible by providing welcome and hospitality to the pilgrims. In the old days of the great medieval pilgrimages, this was very well organized. Today, it would be most helpful if the well-known pilgrimage sites could inform people about the hostels and rest-stations that are especially dedicated to the reception of pilgrims. Just finding lodging in a hotel is not the same as staying in a place with fellow pilgrims. At each rest-station, one should have the opportunity of resting, eating, praying, contemplating and meeting fellow pilgrims who accompany one on at least a portion of the journey. Each new experience of fellowship will be like a foretaste of the ultimate fellowship at the end of times.

Pilgrimages organized by the church (parish or diocesan)

The pilgrimage is a process that embraces different stages which include the spiritual preparation of the pilgrims before departure, a trip of sufficient time and distance, a considerable stay at the sacred site, and active participation in the various activities of the sacred site. People often go on pilgrimage because they are seeking something which they sense is missing in their lives. Life on today's electronic super-highways of instant information and change makes less and less sense. What do we do with all the information at our disposal? The ultimate questions of meaning and purpose become more and more urgent. Whether people live in a life of plenty or of poverty, whether they are super-educated or illiterate, they sense that something essential is missing in today's world, and the ordinary institutions of religion and education do not seem to have adequate responses. Their ordinary church services and university courses do not seem to respond to the deepest questions and yearnings of their heart. The ancient tradition of pilgrimage emerges as an inviting possibility of illumination.

Pilgrimages should not be just a religious term for pious tourism, as is often the case today. You cannot just visit the site, buy souvenirs, send postcards, attend mass and leave! A pilgrimage is not just another trip. It cannot be rushed, and the very rhythm of the pilgrimage should be totally different from the ordinary rhythm of life. Just as some activities will be most helpful, a time for 'holy idleness' will also be necessary for one to come into contact and communion with one's true self. It is a time of personal freedom, a time away from home, friends and relatives, a time of discovery of different places, customs, languages, persons and human situations; it is a time of discernment and illumination, and it is a privileged time of hearing the word of God which throughout the pilgrimage will come in many diverse forms, experiences and persons. At a time when our personal calendars seem to be ever more charged and crowded with many pressing yet ultimately insignificant affairs, the 'time away' will be a sacred journey into the depths of one's self, society and God's creation and equally a journey beyond the limits of one's ordinary vision and concerns. It is a journey both to the very innermost depths of one's being and to the outermost limits of all existence – to inner space and to outer space.

A pilgrimage can be a unique experience of separation and intimacy which are two of the deepest yearnings of the human heart – often in conflict with each other, yet both yearning for fulfilment. Intimacy needs the space of separation in order to grow, appreciate, mature and deepen the relationship with others, while separation needs the bonds of intimacy so that it will not lead to depressing loneliness and spiritual death. If there is to be a true pilgrimage, sufficient time should be devoted to allow for separation from the ordinary routine of life so as to have plenty of time to spend with oneself apart from the others; yet there should also be sufficient time to spend with the others: visiting, singing, searching, joking, eating together, relaxing and equally fasting together; praying, contemplating, listening to the cries and testimonies, hearing the stories of this particular site and why it is a privileged manifestation of the sacred, listening to the word of God, and celebrating especially the sacraments of reconciliation and eucharist. Reconciliation is a moment when distance and closeness meet as one breaks with the past and embraces a new spiritual reality of communion with God, neighbours and the cosmos, and this new reality is celebrated in the eucharist.

In the very separation from the ordinary persons and engagements of everyday life, it is possible to discover a new and deeper level of intimacy with one's inner self – something which is often missing in life and which keeps us from entering into true intimacy even with the ones we love the most. If we cannot be intimate with our inner self, we will not be able to enter into truly intimate relations with others. The newly experienced sense of intimacy within myself will allow me, upon my return home, to enter into new levels of intimacy with the very persons whom I love but had been growing distant from. The positive experience of separation during the pilgrimage can be the very passage into new forms and levels of intimacy when I return home.

The pilgrimage is not a time for a doctrinal or moralistic catechesis, but rather a time for the catechesis of the heart which will come through new profoundly human experiences of friendships, relationships, wonder, gratitude, peace and joy. The pilgrimage is not so much a solution to life's problems or an answer to life's questions as an illuminative and liberating initiation into the mysterious journey of life. This experience of the living word of God as it is seen, experienced and heard through these various sources will help the pilgrim to re-image his/her own life in the true image and likeness of God. Through this re-imaging of oneself, one can gradually discern the sacred meaning and purpose of one's life, and of one's people. Our own historical journey with all its joys and tragedies, successes and failures, convictions and doubts, vice and virtue thus becomes the sacred journey that life truly is. This is not a time for apologies or regrets any more than it is a time for boasting, bragging, or argumentation, but a time for discovering the closeness within the distance, the timeliness within the timelessness, the unlimited within the limits of place and time, the sacred within the human, the divine within the ordinary and the eternal within the temporal. It is a time of coming to grips with the mysterious complexities of life which will never be resolved but which can be accepted, assumed, transcended and celebrated in a totally new way, that is, in the total submission to the divine will which, far from being a dehumanizing surrender, is the beginning of communion with the infinite and with the infinite possibilities of life. This transforming illumination could well be the greatest miracle of the pilgrimage.

The Bible itself is the best example of how every single aspect of life – the heroic and the scandalous, the weak and the strong, the virtuous and the sinful – becomes an integral fibre in the mosaic of God's revelation. Meditating on the scriptures in the light of the footsteps of my own trail can certainly lead to an illumination of the mind and the heart that will transform me from within. This illumination takes place not through some sort of thunder and lightning from heaven, but in the very sharing with others throughout the pilgrimage. Through the process, the clarifying light of God's grace gradually comes through, removes the cataracts of the soul, and allows me to see in the totally unsuspected ways of God!

Seriousness is not opposed to happiness and prayerfulness is not opposed to joyfulness. Fun should not be alien to pilgrimages, since they should be a foretaste of the unending happiness of heaven. Humour and laughter are two of God's greatest gifts to humanity. Through the struggles and sacrifices of the pilgrimage, joyfulness and light-heartedness should equally shine forth. A dull and laughless pilgrimage would not be a Christian one, any more than one that is mere fun and games with no time for reflection, prayer, repentance, insight, transformation and contemplation. The balance of seriousness and fun will make for a true pilgrimage. The total experience of the pilgrimage can help each participant to become more human by coming closer to God, to other human beings, and to other cultural and linguistic expressions of humanity.

Pastoral ministry at the sacred site

Everything about the sacred site should help the pilgrim to achieve a true moment of passage – passage from previous concerns, idolatrous convictions, limited viewpoints to a new and deeper understanding and appreciation of life in all its mysterious complexities. Arrival at the pilgrimage site is best initiated by a gathering mass in which the pilgrims can be welcomed and introduced into the spirit and possibilities of the place. Ample opportunities should be provided so that the pilgrims can participate in the various celebrations of the faith. The entire complex of the sacred site is important with its natural terrain, its walking paths, reflection spaces, devotional sites and central unifying shrine. The pilgrims should be encouraged to see and appreciate the natural terrain – whether beautiful mountains, desolate land, the great plains or whatever it may be – which is the very first revelation of God's presence, beauty and goodness. The very architecture, lay-out of the buildings, art-work and decorations can lead one to a great appreciation of the creative works of men and women who are made in the image of the creative God. But precisely because the pilgrimage site is a place of gathering together totally diverse persons from all backgrounds and walks of life, persons who are complete strangers to one another and even people who would never gather together at home, it can be a graced opportunity for becoming aware of other persons and their human situation – the handicapped, the infirm, the refugees, the 'untouchables' of any society, and many others. In discovering ourselves to be in community with others, even total strangers, we experience the ultimate reality of the church as the people of God who has no boundaries and is open to everyone without exception. There should be ample opportunities for the pilgrims to meet one another and have good fraternal experiences among strangers. This will be a 'mini' but powerful experience in what church-building should be about. This experience which is seen and lived can expand and deepen our appreciation of the church itself.

During medieval times, great plays were often organized for the education and edification of pilgrims. Often the porticos of the churches were adorned with the various scenes from the Bible so as to instruct the faithful. This same spirit can be carried out today through the use of modern media: videos, photo and multi-media exhibits. Scenes of the last judgment of Matthew can be correlated with scenes which bring out the plight of the poor, the abandoned, the imprisoned and the starving of this world. Because people come with a predisposition to meet others, the exhibitions of the pilgrimage site can help the pilgrims to come into contact with the others from home or from other nations who might not be immediately obvious: the sickly, the dirty, undernourished, the crippled, the homeless, the abandoned children or elderly, and everyone whom the ordinary world keeps well hidden, could be made present and visible. Everything should help pilgrims to develop a deeper sensitivity to their sisters and brothers in need.

Within this context of encounter, there should be plenty of opportunities for silence and reflection; meaningful devotions, especially the Way of the Cross; and sacramental reconciliation with compassionate confessors for those who want truly to cleanse themselves and make a new beginning; and good liturgies with good singing and preaching that truly speaks to the quest of the pilgrims. The departing eucharist should be the true highlight of the pilgrimage and not just a ritual which appears as a necessary but uninspiring moment of the process. It should bring the process to a climax and send the pilgrims forth with a renewed and even restored sense of faith, hope and apostolic zeal. No one should leave for home as they departed from home! The end of the pilgrimage mass should be a true missionary mandate for those who have been transformed and given new life through the process of the pilgrimage.

Pilgrimages do not replace the ordinary ministries of the church, but they can certainly be privileged experiences which can be sources of new life both for the individual faithful and for the church itself. Precisely because they are not necessary or mandated, they can be moments of spiritual freedom enabling great marvels to take place in the lives of men and women. When the church accompanies the pilgrims in the proper way, its services can serve as catalysts to the many wonders which God will bring about.

Notes

1. Many of the ideas for this article have been taken from the author's own pastoral experience and from '*Un pèlerinage c'est exigeant*' prepared by L'Association Nationale des Directeurs de Pèlerinages, 10 Place Claudinon Giraudet, 42500 Le Chambon Feugerolles, France.

The Interpretation of a Mystic: St John of the Cross

Michel de Godet

Since St John of the Cross's sole aim in the *Ascent of Mount Carmel* is to help contemplatives to move towards union with God, one would not expect him to show the least interest in pilgrimages. He maintains the tradition that here below we are 'pilgrims' on a journey to the world beyond, 'poor, in exile, orphans, carrying nothing on the way'.[1] Such pilgrims, with no other guide than the 'light burning in their heart',[2] aspire in all things to live in the 'abiding city' (Heb. 13.14). So it is all the more remarkable that the mystical Doctor includes among the means which God uses to arouse 'devotion' in the will places which he describes as 'devotional'.[3] In one short chapter he presents a substantial theology of spiritual practice associated with places which God allows or wants us to engage in.

St John of the Cross distinguishes three kinds of place. There are places 'which look pleasant and naturally arouse devotion'. Three elements or aspects of them are emphasized: the disposition of the ground, the trees, and a quiet loneliness; in other words, the background which makes them an attractive setting for solitary meditation. Here we may recognize traces of personal experience – that of the Novice Master out walking and choosing places where the young religious entrusted to him can feel drawn to praise the Creator, together with the long hours of prayer passed on the hillsides dominating the convent in Segovia, heights from which one can watch the swaying pine trees combing up the slopes of Mont Valsain, for much of the year covered with snow. Once wrapt in meditation, the religious leaves behind the 'means' which has facilitated this. He is then 'in the presence of God within', and absent from the place where he is physically.

During those nights in Segovia, the experience of darkness which affected his whole being in the world became a unique symbol of the experience of the night of faith which similarly affected all his being, though of course in a very different way. Such symbolism became possible for John of the Cross only by a quite exceptional inner reciprocity between his poetic gifts and his mystical grace. In his case, the statement that some places naturally arouse devotion in no way points towards a nature mysticism; rather, it evokes the relationship which becomes established between the creature and the infinitely generous presence of God in his creative Word, when purity of heart resounds in harmony with it, in humble praise and thanksgiving. In that case any reference to 'nature' denotes the spontaneous character of what arises from a strictly mystical encounter.

The places of the second kind are those where God is accustomed to communicate to God's friends 'spiritual graces of exceeding sweetness'. Here the link between the place and the grace is simply that the religious feels drawn to return to such a place. If the grace of God does not in any way depend on conditions of time and space, as John of the Cross forcibly recalls, doesn't this attraction seem suspiciously like indulgence? Doesn't its source lie in a desire to appropriate the gifts of God? The ways of God taught by experience do not have this exclusive and suspicious rigour. There are three justifications for the attraction that the place has on the soul which feels touched by God there.

1. 'It appears that God wills that he should be glorified there.' Where other spiritual writers would see a concession by God to the weakness of the soul, St John of the Cross's emphasis is primarily on the will of God.

2. The soul often finds it easier to remember to thank God more easily in the place where it receives grace.

3. This remembrance, facilitated by presence in the place, leads to greater devotion.

Here we can see how deeply sacramental St John of the Cross's view is. Human beings belong to a world of the senses, or more precisely are subjects formed by emerging from this world. The matter of the sacrament – here the place – conveys nothing to faith: it only 'speaks' if a word is inscribed on it that is audible to faith. The place where a subject has received a grace from God says nothing of this grace in itself; the grace needs no specific location. However, once the place becomes a vehicle of spiritual communication for the subject, it also becomes as it were the sacrament of a relationship which is open to confirmation, if God wills to confirm his gift along the course which he has already freely taken.

Confirmation will be given by living memory, the memory which God himself keeps awake or seeks to arouse. This is not so that the contemplative can satisfy a desire for repetition, and therefore possession, but so that the first grace can blossom into thanksgiving. In effect God wants thanksgiving because it, and it alone, allows him to share his possession with the creature whom he has made in his likeness.

St John of the Cross's prayer in Segovia seems to identify the first two kinds of places of devotion: the saint is led to devotion by the disposition of the ground, and he feels driven to return, when he has the leisure, to a particular cave in which spiritual graces are renewed. It is as if God wanted to make use of a conspiracy between the beauties of his creation and this new Poverello in order to fill the saint's heart with perfect joy.[4]

Having recalled, in order to avoid all ambiguity, that the soul is the only place which is pleasing to God, St John of the Cross can choose from the scriptures three examples of veneration of a place which memory associates with a divine communication: 'Abraham built an altar in the place where God appeared to him, and there called upon His name, and he visited the place again on his return from Egypt, and called upon God again there at the altar which he had made before. Jacob also consecrated the place where he saw the Lord leaning upon the ladder; for he took the stone which he had laid under his head, and set it up for a title, pouring oil upon the top of it. Hagar, too, in reverence gave a name to the place where the Angel appeared to her, saying, "Truly here I have seen the hinder parts of the One who sees me."'

The third kind of place consists in particular places 'which God has chosen so that he can be called upon and served there', like Sinai, 'where God gave the law to Moses'; Moriah, which God showed to Abraham as a place 'where he was to sacrifice his son'; and Mount Horeb. Here St John of the Cross uses the name used in I Kings for the mountain on which God showed himself to Elijah. Two other examples have been taken from the Christian tradition. As in the case of the places mentioned by scripture, the choice of place is not a human one; but instead of being attributed to God himself, as is the case with the biblical places cited above, here it is attributed to the saints of God: St Michael dedicated Mount Garganus, where an oratory was dedicated to God in honour of the angels; the most glorious Virgin chose a place in Rome for the building of a church in her honour.

Unlike the first kind of places, which serve only to arouse 'devotion', and the second kind of places, which become 'places of devotion' only through the living memory that the contemplative can maintain by grace received, the places of this third kind are chosen by God or by his saints for crowds of believers to visit in order to express their prayers and praises. St John of the Cross does not dwell on the fact that in the three examples taken from the scriptures it is primarily the individual who receives the grace of a divine manifestation; he presupposes that this grace is primarily destined to make a place, with a view to a common expression of faith. On the case of both Sinai and Horeb, the communications received by Moses and Elijah relate to the whole people of God. Thus the children of Israel seem to be to all intents and purposes invited to come to these places, there to recall the gift received by a mediator or a prophet. Saint John of the Cross fails to mention, or is ignorant of, the fact that we do not have any biblical or Jewish evidence for any kind of pilgrimage in the footsteps of these who one day were to appear alongside Christ on the Mount of the Transfigura- tion. The mystical Doctor perhaps had in mind the building of the temple on Mount Moriah (according to a tradition echoed in II Chron. 3.1), and all the pilgrimages of the 'ascents' to the house of the Lord which it attracted. He also certainly knew of the Christian pilgrimages to Mount Sinai and the presence there of the monks of St Catherine's monastery.

An outline interpretation

With its concern for practice, this spiritual theology of pilgrimage did not pause to reflect on its options or its foundations. Here I shall try briefly to elucidate some of them.

A divine choice

It is only in connection with the third category that John of the Cross asks, 'What is the reason why God chose these places?' A theologian trained in Salamanca, the Mystical Doctor knows that the way in which God disposes of his grace to communicate with human beings is truly intelligible to the believer. The elements in this economy are held together by a unity which is affirmed only by and in faith; however, it is a real connection which is thoroughly rational, in the light of faith. This quest for fitting reasons here ends up in failure, or rather in an avowal which is praise of the unfathomable wisdom of God: 'God alone knows why he chose these places, rather than others, to be praised in. All we need to know is that all is for our good.' Here we find the same humility as that of the theologian faced with the fact that God does not lead to contemplation all those who give themselves to prayer: 'God alone knows the reason.'[5] Thus the theological sense of John of the Cross when confronted by the 'fact' of pilgrimages is intensified: these are the object of a divine choice, a choice which reason cannot explain. The one who submits humbly to God's choice finds there is a way of God. One could be tempted to suspect that this theology endorses some kind of divine interventionism. However, that would fail to recognize that St John of the Cross is particularly attentive to human mediations, to the human dimension in which providence is active. When God inclines hearts, he allows them to share in the freedom of his choice, though that does not mean that they do not have to pass through times of trial. Here the life and mission of Bernadette Soubirous remain a humble and marvellous witness.

The 'reception' of pilgrimages in the life of the church

The church recognizes the gifts which God gives it. Who can discern the spirits, if not the bride of Christ, in whom his Spirit of truth dwells? Who can be certain of a 'divine choice', if faith does not establish it in the primordial choice which God has made of the body of his Son? It is in this body that we are made alive in the communion of the Holy Spirit. St John of the Cross says of the graces which can adorn the course of the spiritual life that when they truly come from God, they themselves incline the one who receives them to submit to the judgment of the one to whom they are said.[6] Though he has just said that prayer is not bound to any place, St John of the Cross emphasizes that in places dedicated to the worship of God, 'there is far greater reason why we should be heard' because the church has 'consecrated them for that special end'.

Incarnate memory. Holy places or places of holy memory?

Both the second and the third kind of place of devotion which John of the Cross identifies suggest that the memory of the gifts of God needs to find a trace of them in the places where they have been received. Is this a weakness which prevents us from worshipping God, no longer in this place or that, but in spirit and in truth (cf. John 4.23–24)? Doesn't St Paul remind us that everything which distinguishes, particularizes or is in conflict ceases to exist in Christ? 'There is no longer Jew nor Greek, slave nor free, male nor female, for you are all one in Christ Jesus' (Gal. 3.28). However, in Christ, the Jews and the Greeks (a term using the part for the whole, namely the nations) are reconciled only in the 'remnant' which has believed in the gospel (Rom. 11.6); the destiny of the 'others' (Rom. 11.7) is the subject of three chapters in Romans. In Christ, man and woman are the beneficiaries of a sacrament; the poor, who can be compared with the 'slave' of Gal. 3.27, represents Christ in the eyes of believers in an almost sacramental way. Thus, even if there are no longer privileged places for encountering God, there is still room for an incarnation of memory in the places which preserve the traces of a passing for the keen eye of memory and for it alone. Holy places or places of holy memory? Places of holy memory, excluding all sacralization of places, no matter where they may be. Places of holy memory, places where believers can recall a living memory: it is here, at a particular banal or dramatic moment of our life, that the Saviour came to visit us, going about and doing good (cf. Acts 10.38).

Translated by John Bowden

Notes

1. For the works of St John of the Cross see *The Complete Works of St John of the Cross* (3 vols.), translated and edited by E. Allison Peers, London 1934–5.
2. 'Poem of the Dark Night', third stanza.
3. *The Ascent of Mount Carmel*, ch. 42. Unless otherwise indicated, all quotations are from this chapter.
4. Here we might recall, with the Spiritual Canticle, the 'graces' spread through creation by the 'passage' of the creative Word.
5. *The Dark Night*, 1, 9, 9.
6. *The Ascent of Mount Carmel*, II, 22,9; 22,16.

Contributors

PAUL POST was born in 1953 and studied theology at the Catholic Theological University in Utrecht, where he gained his doctorate in 1984, and Christian art and archaeology at the Pontifical Institute of Christian Archaeology in Rome. After lecturing in liturgy and sacramental theology at the Catholic Theological University in Heerlen from 1980 until 1988, he was head of the Department of Folklore and European Ethnology at the P. J. Moertens Institute, part of the Royal Netherlands Academy of Arts and Sciences until 1994. Since then he has been Professor of Liturgy and Sacramental Theology at the Theological Faculty of Tilburg and Director of the Liturgical Institute there. His main interests are in the field of liturgy, popular religion and Christian art, particularly in recent developments. He has written numerous books and articles.

DAVID CARRASCO is Professor of History of Religions, Director of the Mesoamerican Archive, and Master of Mathey College at Princeton University. He has written numerous articles and monographs, including *Quetzalcoatl and the Irony of Empire* (1982 and 1991) and *Religions of Mesoamerica* (1990); and is joint author of *Waiting for the Dawn: Mircea Eliade in Perspective* (1986 and 1991), *The Great Temple of Tenochtitlan* (1987), and *Moctezuma's Mexico* (1992); he has edited *The Imagination of Matter* (1989) and *To Change Place* (1991), and is currently chief editor of the *Oxford Encyclopedia of Mesoamerican Cultures*, a multi-volume reference work to be published in 1999. For over twenty years he has taught classes and lectured widely on New World religions, millenarian movements, city and symbol in comparative perspective, colonialism and ceremony, and theory and method in the study of religion. His research interests include comparative studies of sacred landscapes, ceremonial centres, myth, ritual performance, religious imagination, cultural discourse in the Americas, and Latin American and Chicana/o literature, music, and visual arts.

Address: Princeton University, Department of Religion, Seventy-Nine Hall, Princeton, New Jersey 08544–1006, USA.

SEAN FREYNE is Professor of Theology at Trinity College, Dublin and is a member of the editorial board of *Concilium*. He has written a number of scholarly books and articles on New Testament themes with a special emphasis on Galilean life and culture within the context of Second Temple Judaism.

Address: 24 Charleville Road, Rathmines, Dublin 6, Ireland.

JAIME R. VIDAL was born in Ponce, Puerto Rico, in 1943. He went to the United States for his studies, obtaining a PhD in Theology from Fordham University in 1984. He was Assistant Director of the Cushwa Center for the Study of American Catholicism, at the University of Notre Dame, from 1990 to 1994, during which time he also taught Christian Spirituality at Notre Dame's Theology Department. Since 1994 he has been Director of Hispanic Studies at the School of Theology of the Pontifical College Josephinum, Columbus, Ohio. He co-edited the second volume of the *Notre Dame History of US Hispanic Catholics*, under the title *Puerto Rican and Cuban Catholics in the US: 1900–1965*, Notre Dame, Indiana 1994, and wrote the article 'Citizens, yet Strangers: the Puerto Rican Experience' in it (pp. 11–132).

Address: 38 East New England Avenue, Worthington, OH 43085, USA.

RAIMON PANIKKAR, who this year celebrates the golden jubilee of his priestly ordination, after a life dedicated to his ministry (mainly among intellectuals) and an academic activity as Professor of Religious Studies (now Emeritus from the University of California), continues a contemplative life retired in a small village of the pre-Pyrenees with occasional journeys to India and other parts of the world. Among his forty books are *Invisible Harmony*, Minneapolis 1995; *Il daimôn della politica*, Bologna 1995; *The Vedic Experience*, Delhi 1994; *The Cosmotheandric Experience*, Maryknoll 1993; *La Trinidad y la experiencia religiosa*, Barcelona 1989; *Myth, Faith and Hermeneutics*, Bangalore 1983, etc. Forthcoming is *La experiencia filosófica de la India*, Madrid 1996.

Address: Can Felo, 08511 Tavertet (Catalunya), Spain.

PHILIPPE BAUD was born in Vevey, Switzerland in 1942, studied theology at the major seminary in Fribourg, and then gained a degree in theology at the Institut catholique in Paris. A diocesan priest, for sixteen years he was engaged in pastoral ministry in a large parish in Geneva, on the liturgy of which he has left his stamp. Since 1984 he has been in charge of the Catholic chaplaincy of the University and Federal Polytechnic of Lausanne. In 1985 he founded the Catholic Study Centre of Lausanne, where he has welcomed a variety of public figures, both religious and secular. His books include: *Premier épître aux techniciens* (with Jacques Neirynck), Lausanne 1989; *Nicolas de Flue. Une silence qui fonde la Suisse*, Paris 1993; *Prier avec l'Ancien Testament*, Paris 1994; *Prier avec le Nouveau Testament*, Paris 1994; *Le chemin de croix. Les origines d'une dévotion populaire*, Paris 1995.

Address: Alumônerie Universitaire Catholique, 31 Bd de Grancy, CH-1006 Lausanne, Switzerland.

JOSE OSCAR BEOZZO was born in Santa Adelia (SP), Brazil, in 1941, and ordained priest in the diocese of Lins in 1964. He studied philosophy in São Paulo, theology at the Gregorian in Rome, sociology and social communication at the Catholic University of Louvain. He is executive secretary of CESEP (Ecumenical Centre for Services to Evangelization and Popular Education), a member of the executive board of CEHILA (Commission for Study of Church History in Latin America) and a lecturer at the theology faculty of São Paulo University. His publications include *Trabalho, crise e alternativas* (1995); *Igreja no Brasil: de João XXIII a João Paulo II* (1995); and, as editor for the Brazil area, *Historia do Concilio Vaticano II* (1995).

Address: Rua Oliveira Alves 164, São Paulo (SP) 04210–060, Brazil.

PAUL J. PHILIBERT, OP, was born in Baltimore, Maryland, in 1936 and is a Dominican priest. He holds a licentiate and a doctorate in theology from the Dominican Pontifical Faculty in Washington, DC. At the University of Notre Dame (USA) he is Director of the Institute for Church Life. He has written various articles on moral development and spirituality in books and journals and recently edited *Living in the Meantime: Concerning the Transformation of Religious Life* (1994) and written *Seeing and Believing* (1995).

Address: Institute for Church Life, 1201 Hesburgh Library, Notre Dame, Indiana 46556, USA.

ALEX GARCÍA-RIVERA is a native of Havana, Cuba, and a Roman Catholic lay theologian. He received his doctorate in theology from the Lutheran

School of Theology at Chicago and holds degrees in physics from Ohio State University and Miami University. The author of numerous articles and winner of two Catholic Press Association awards, he is assistant professor of systematic theology at the Jesuit School of Theology at Berkeley. His most recent publications include *St Martin de Porres: The 'Little Stories' and the Semiotics of Culture*, Maryknoll 1995, and 'Religious Imagination', in *Perspectivas: Hispanic Ministry*, ed. Allan Figueroa Deck, Timothy M. Matovina, and Yolanda Tarango, Kansas City 1995, 94–7.

Address: Jesuit School of Theology, 1735 LeRoy Avenue, Berkeley, Cal. 94709, USA.

VIRGIL ELIZONDO was born in San Antonio, Texas, and studied at the Ateneo University and the East Asian Pastoral Institute, Manila, and at the Institut Catholique, Paris. Since 1971 he has been President of the Mexican American Cultural Center in San Antonio. He has published numerous books and articles and has been on the editorial board of *Concilium, Catequesis Latino Americana* and the *God With Us Catechetical Series*. He does much theological reflection with the grass-roots people in the poor neighbourhoods of the USA.

Address: Mexican Cultural Centre, 3019 W. French Pl, PO Box 28185, San Antonio, Texas 78205, USA.

MICHEL DE GODET is a Discalced Carmelite. He was born in 1924 and ordained priest in 1949 and has published articles in exegesis, theology and spirituality. His books include *Le Christ de Thérèse de Jésus*, Paris 1993, and *Le Christ de Jean de la Croix*, Paris 1994.

Address: 5 Villa de la Réunion, 75016 Paris, France.

Members of the Advisory Committee for Spirituality

Directors

Christian Duquoc OP	Lyons	France
Virgil Elizondo	San Antonio	United States

Members

Philippe Baud	Lausanne	Switzerland
Frei Betto	Sao Paulo SP	Brazil
Enzo Bianchi	Magnano	Italy
Carolo Carozzo	Genoa	Italy
Keith Egan	Notre Dame	United States
Casiano Floristan	Madrid	Spain
Michel de Godet OCD	Vaux-sous-Chèvremont	Belgium
Gustavo Gutiérrez	Lima	Peru
Camilo Maccise OCD	Rome	Italy
Christianne Méroz	Woudsend	The Netherlands
	and Grandchamp	Switzerland
Sebastian Painadath SJ	Kerala	India
Jan Peters OCD	Smakt	The Netherlands
Paul Philibert	Notre Dame	United States
Armido Rizzi	Fiesole	Italy
Samuel Ruiz	Chiapas	Mexico
Pedro Trigo	Caracas	Venezuela

Directors-Counsellors – cont.

Mercy Amba Oduyoye	Princeton	USA
John Panagnopoulos	Athens	Greece
Aloysius Pieris SJ	Gonawala-Kelaniya	Sri Lanka
James Provost	Washington, DC	USA
Giuseppe Ruggieri	Catania	Italy
Christoph Theobald SJ	Paris	France
Miklós Tomka	Budapest	Hungary
David Tracy	Chicago, IL	USA
Marciano Vidal CSSR	Madrid	Spain
Knut Walf	Nijmegen	The Netherlands

General Secretariat: Prins Bernardstraat 2, 6521 A B Nijmegen, The Netherlands
Manager: Mrs E. C. Duindam-Deckers

Some Back Issues of *Concilium* still available

All listed issues published before 1991 are available at £6.95 each. Issues published after 1991 are £8.95 each. Add 10% of value for postage.
US, Canadian and Philippian subscribers contact: Orbis Books, Shipping Dept., Maryknoll, NY 10545 USA

Special rates are sometimes available for large orders. Please write for details.

Please send orders and remittances to:
SCM Press Ltd, 9–17 St Albans Place, London N1 0NX

Concilium Subscription Information
- outside North America

Individual Annual Subscription (1996 six issues): £30.00

Institution Annual Subscription (1996 six issues): £40.00

Airmail subscriptions: add £10.00

Individual issues: £8.95 each

New subscribers please return this form:
for a two-year subscription, double the appropriate rate

1996 *Concilium* subscriptions   ☐   £30.00   ....
(for individuals)

1996 *Concilium* subscriptions   ☐   £40.00   ....
(for institutions)

For airmail postage outside Europe   ☐   + £10.00   ....
(optional) please add £10.00

Total   . . . .

I wish to subscribe for one/two years as an individual/institution
(delete as appropriate)

Name . . . .

Address . . . .

. . . .

. . . . Postcode . . . .

I enclose a cheque for . . . . made payable to SCM Press Ltd

Please charge my Access/Visa/Mastercard No . . . . / . . . . / . . . . / . . . .

Signature . . . . Expiry Date . . . .

Please send this form to:
SCM Press Ltd (Concilium) 9-17 St Albans Place London N1 0NX
Credit card telephone orders on: 0171-359 8033   Fax: 0171-359 0049

CONCILIUM

The Theological Journal of the 1990s

Now available from Orbis Books

...nded in 1965 and published six times a year, *Concilium* is a world-wide ...nal of theology. Its editors and essayists encompass a veritable 'who's ...' of theological scholars. Not only the greatest names in Catholic theology, ...ut exciting new voices from every part of the world, have written for this unique journal.

Concilium exists to promote theological discussion in the spirit of Vatican II, out of which it was born. It is a catholic journal in the widest sense: rooted firmly in the Catholic heritage, open to other Christian traditions and the world's faiths. Each issue of *Concilium* focusses on a theme of crucial importance and the widest possible concern for our time. With contributions from Asia, Africa, North and South America, and Europe, *Concilium* truly reflects the multiple facets of the world church.

Now available from Orbis Books, *Concilium* will continue to focus theological debate and to challenge scholars and students alike.